Living a Leadership Lifestyle

A Guide for New and Aspiring Leaders

Ross Emerson

Leader in applied, concise business books

Living a Leadership Lifestyle: A Guide for New and Aspiring Leaders

First published in 2023 by
Business Expert Press, LLC
222 East 46th Street, New York, NY 10017
www.businessexpertpress.com

ISBN-13: 978-1-63742-481-0 (paperback)
ISBN-13: 978-1-63742-482-7 (e-book)

Business Expert Press Human Resource Management and Organizational Behavior Collection

First edition: 2023

10 9 8 7 6 5 4 3 2 1

Living a Leadership Lifestyle

*This book is dedicated to all the aspiring leaders who find
the motivation and courage to live their leadership
lifestyle daily
and
for the future leadership lifestylers whom I had in my
mind as I wrote this book:
Matthew Henriques
Brian Henriques
Kristen Smith
Trevor Smith
Benjamin D'Mello*

Description

Living a Leadership Lifestyle is a different type of leadership book that approaches leadership from a unique perspective. Rather than focusing on specific leadership skills, this book argues that successful leadership begins by *living* leadership as a lifestyle and having leadership mindsets that guide decisions and behaviors daily.

After describing his own leadership journey and personal leadership quest across continents and cultures, the author shares 13 key insights for living a leadership lifestyle, including:

- Build and protect your personal leadership brand.
- Failure is opportunity in disguise.
- Be courageous and carve your own path.

Living a Leadership Lifestyle is a pragmatic book demonstrating the characteristics of good leadership essential for aspiring leaders. By developing and harnessing the leadership mindsets shared, readers will self-administer a "tonic" for the challenges life brings nurturing the resilience, self-awareness, and courage required to help readers carve their own path to success.

Keywords

leadership; success; lifestyle; personal development; professional development

Contents

Testimonials

"It was a pleasure to read this book. It definitely shows a different side of leadership. Most often than not, accounts of leadership stories, and leadership manuals refer to C-level very prominent executives or high-rank politicians, who are not really the average leader or that don't really lead in the average context. In that sense, this book contains a narrative much closer to rest of us, and also allows us to better empathize with the author and his advice, because his story seems closer and more similar to the rest of us.

This book invites us to take ownership of ourselves, our lives, and our careers. Through an engaging narrative of his professional life, the author shows how our inner leader has to be empowered not by cliché 'do-it-this-way' lists, but through a constant dialogue with our core values, and by embracing a leadership lifestyle of endless learning. The insights of this book tell a different story of leadership, away from the shining spotlight chronicles of constant success, and closer to the reality of the roller-coaster journey that being a resilient leader entails."—**David Lopez Batista, Strategy, International Management and Entrepreneurship Department, King's Business School, King's College London**

"In what can only be described as a candid and refreshingly personal take on the subject, this leadership book stands out as the most honest and straightforward I have ever encountered.

Divided into two parts, the first follows the author's own turbulent journey as an exemplar of the leadership lifestyle, a poignant reminder of the interconnectedness of our personal and professional lives. As the author astutely points out, neglecting one at the expense of the other is a sure recipe for failure.

Part two presents thirteen invaluable insights into how one can connect with their inner voice and values to achieve the right balance in life. Drawing heavily from the author's own experiences, this section reads like a manual, making it easy and enjoyable to follow the author's journey and make meaningful *connections with one's own experiences. Each insight concludes with a practical summary and an easy-to-use tool that the reader can apply immediately.*

It is my firm belief that everyone should read this book, regardless of their circumstances or station in life. The insights contained herein are powerful and can change your personal and professional mindset in profound ways.

By taking ownership of one's own self, life, and career, the book inspires the courage to embrace change and follow one's passion, no matter the obstacles. If you are looking for a travel companion on your journey to self-discovery, this book is your best bet."—**Birgitte Kreiborg, Mother of two and founding partner of a Multi Family Office in Monaco**

"Reading this book gave me the motivation and mindset I needed to pursue my goals and strive for the success I know I am capable of achieving!" —**Shannon Robertson, Director of Delivery Enablement, North America ICEO Leadership Practice, LHH**

Acknowledgments

- Thank you to my mother, Margaret, and my older sister, Erika, who always supported me throughout my life and gave me the freedom and scope to carve out my life's path and live my leadership lifestyle in my own way.
- Thank you to all the mentors I have had the privilege of meeting along my own journey. You supported me, guided me, helped me, challenged me, and on many occasions traveled with me as I learned about my own leadership and settled into my own leadership lifestyle.
- Thank you to my editor, Chris Murray. You helped me to organize my thoughts better and get my ideas across more effectively and you were the calming voice of experience I valued so very much through the writing of this very personal book and sharing of my life story.
- Thank you to my dear friend and confidante, Shannon (Starlight) Robertson, for the graphics illustrations appearing at the start of each Insight.
- Thank you to Claudio Lenci at OCRE officina di creatività (ocre.com.br). You helped to bring the vision in my mind to life with your compelling and uplifting cover design.
- Thank you to my publisher, Scott Isenberg, and the team at the Business Expert Press. You saw something different and interesting in my own views and mindset of leadership as a lifestyle that anyone can choose and gave me the opportunity to share my perspectives with others through this book.

Introduction

Bookstores of all types are flooded with books on leadership, from classic how-to books such as John Kotter's *Leading Change* or Warren Bennis's *On Becoming a Leader*, to the "leadership lessons" of famous business leaders, politicians, and even explorers (*Shackleton's Way* was a bestseller). Many of these books have great insight into the skills needed to be an effective leader. This book, *Living a Leadership Lifestyle*, is a different type of leadership book that approaches leadership from a unique perspective. Rather than focusing on specific leadership skills, such as how to inspire employees or how to communicate more effectively, this book uses the premise that successful leadership begins by having a leadership mindset that guides your decisions and behaviors so they are integrated seamlessly in your day-to-day personal as well as professional life and in essence, enables you to live a leadership lifestyle.

Through this approach, leadership becomes readily and easily accessible to anyone who aspires to leadership, regardless of age, stage, ability, or circumstance. Anyone can develop and live a leadership lifestyle daily with a bit of conscious and considered practice. With this mindset and a commitment to live a leadership lifestyle, the journey to success becomes much more attainable to all who choose to pursue the path in this manner. No longer will you be comparing yourself to others and competing for the rewards dictated by society. Instead, you will *go within* and compete with yourself to become the best you possible, resourcefully using the insights in this book to become a success regardless of how you define it. The journey to living a leadership lifestyle is liberating, empowering, meaningful, … and fun.

One of the things that gives me a great deal of satisfaction is helping others to avoid the kinds of mistakes I made through my own life—and there were many. But through those mistakes made over the years, I picked up vital insights for success by being open-minded to learning and finding courage along the way to go down some paths that others may not choose for themselves. A strong theme that has influenced my own leadership development is reflection. Deep reflection always helped me gain new awareness and different perspectives of the challenges I faced and overcame time and time again.

This book will show you how thinking of leadership as a consciously chosen lifestyle will help you develop the leadership skills, attributes, and perspectives that are essential for success in today's complex and rapidly evolving world. A consciously chosen leadership lifestyle involves adopting a set of healthy mindsets and behaviors that when used regularly and continuously in daily life, regardless of the setting, will help develop valuable leadership skills for everyday life and for success in the workplace.

The key benefit of putting these skills into practice is the ability to nurture resilience and recover from adversity in all its forms. Developing and harnessing these skills is the equivalent of administering yourself a "tonic" for sustainable recovery to the challenges life brings, both in your personal and working lives. This is a pragmatic book demonstrating that the characteristic behaviors of good leadership are the same in working life as they are in daily life, and by living a leadership lifestyle you can put yourself on the path to holistic success.

The book is written in two main parts, each distinct from the other yet connected in the storytelling about living a leadership lifestyle. The first part is called "A Personal Leadership Journey" and is written in the style of a memoir. This section introduces the reader to life-shaping events in a professional and personal journey that took me across three continents, working and living in cities such as Toronto, London, Monte Carlo, and Osaka. My career was equally varied, ranging from working for a non-profit organization that led me to periodic work-related events in Buckingham Palace to managing investment portfolios of the ultrawealthy in Monaco. Every role had its ups and downs, but through the variety of challenges and obstacles I faced in my life and successes that came along the way, I was unconsciously developing valuable leadership lessons.

Facing a series of difficult situations challenged me to deal with and overcome adversity, which helped shape both my personal leadership style and my current perspectives of leadership. Over time, facing more adverse situations, I continued to reflect on the lessons and insights of adversity, from which emerged a conscious awareness of the leader I was becoming—not through any formalized role or title but rather through the way I chose to live my daily life. This growth eventually transformed into my current leadership philosophy that leadership is a lifestyle that people can live by choice.

The second part of the book is called "13 Insights for Living a Leadership Lifestyle" and focuses on 13 mindsets that can be used to develop the readers' own leadership and success skills. Each insight includes specific takeaways that you can use step-by-step to apply the insight in your life and your career. The insights are presented in a sequence that I consider the most effective for learning and better understanding what leadership is about. It is also based on my own journey to living a leadership lifestyle. I employ this sequence in much of the leadership coaching work I do today.

The 13 insights in Part 2 are as follows:

1. You are accountable for your own success.
2. Be self-aware and respond to your feelings.
3. Build and protect your personal brand.
4. Trust your instincts. Listen to your inner voice.
5. Visualize. Plan. Act.
6. Accept that risk is part of a leadership lifestyle.
7. Build your resilience.
8. Failure is just opportunity in disguise.
9. Be courageous and carve your own path.
10. You define progress and success.
11. Celebrate the successes along the way.
12. Be a student of life, and a student for life.
13. Make the difficult choices that are needed.

One of the key messages to take away from this book is that you have to put all these insights into action ... you have to *LIVE* your leadership lifestyle on a regular basis for the leadership growth and development to occur. A leadership lifestyle will fill your life with purpose, meaning, and success in whichever way you define them. Have courage, have faith in yourself, and most importantly as you learn how to live your own leadership lifestyle by reading this book, make sure to have fun!

PART 1

A Personal Leadership Journey

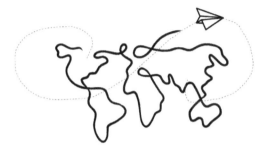

CHAPTER 1

The Twists and Turns of My Early Career Years

My career began after completing my Bachelor of Arts degree in Politics at university followed by a postgraduate certificate in International Business Management. I pursued the certificate because I had no success getting a full-time job after completing my undergraduate degree. So, I tried to be constructive by continuing my learning after the discouraging failure in all my attempts to land a job. Eventually, through my certificate course I was able to secure employment, but there were some compromises and sacrifices to be made because the only job I could get was abroad and this meant I would be far away from my friends and family. But I needed to get on the job ladder so I accepted the position as a gesture of responsibility and acknowledging that I was accountable for my own success. This is an important tenet of living a leadership lifestyle and will be discussed more in Insight 1 in the second part of this book.

My first full-time job took me to Osaka, Japan, for several years. Although this was a wonderful, horizon-broadening opportunity, in some respects it was also a challenging and lonely period. But I tried to make the most of the situation and embrace the new culture I was working in and eventually things improved. In the end, it turned out to be an amazing life-altering experience for me, which was incredibly developmental and a time in my life I will never forget. A few years after I first made my way to Japan, I returned to Canada to continue my studies at the Master level where I completed an MBA with specialties in marketing and strategic management. During this period of graduate study, my path diverged from the usual, conventional path followed by most of the others around me—a pattern that would become one of the defining characteristics of my life, and a core component of a leadership lifestyle.

In January of the second year of my MBA study, I enrolled in a special consulting course that took me into the Arctic Circle to complete a strategy assignment to benefit a First Nations tribe and community in Canada's north. "Wow … what an opportunity!" I thought to myself as I enthusiastically waited for the course to begin. What I didn't think about at the time was just how cold it gets in the Arctic Circle in January—a lesson I'll never forget. I reflected on the opportunity and realized that doing something off the beaten path was a chance to experience something different and learn new things. The assignment lasted about a week and through my time in the frozen north of Canada, I saw the Aurora Borealis (a.k.a. the northern lights), ate caribou and bannock for the first time, got invited to dinner at the house of a genuine First Nations tribal chief, and had an amazingly different learning opportunity that most people never get the chance to experience.

Another opportunity I had during that time was working as a consultant in an MBA student consulting business that was run independently within our business school. I had the chance to apply the concepts I was learning in my degree firsthand while directly making an impact by helping small businesses improve their performance so they could grow and thrive. It was an incredibly fulfilling experience. Working directly with independent business owners and entrepreneurs gave me an appreciation of the many challenges small businesses and entrepreneurs face as they try to launch their businesses or take them to the next level. At times, the opportunities I was getting felt like I was on an amazing winning streak through my graduate student years. But alas, all good things come to an end. While I had the opportunity to have these wonderful experiences, I also had many difficulties through those years and out of necessity, I was forced to work part time for the duration of the program because of financial difficulty. At one stage through my studies, I had to sleep on a couch in my sister's apartment (thank you big sis!) for a year to save money as I put myself through graduate school. I graduated with my MBA later that year and, because of the breadth of experience I had acquired during my graduate studies, I was one of only a handful of graduating students who successfully secured permanent employment prior to graduation. My MBA studies exemplified the combination of opportunity and sacrifice that often emerges on the roads that lead to accomplishment.

Early Career Successes, First Career Challenge … and a High-Risk Decision

I started working at the head office of a large Canadian bank shortly after graduation that summer. I didn't have the luxury of going on a summer holiday as most of my classmates did but at least I had a job lined up and for that I was grateful. It was a sacrifice I was very willing to make and one that I could easily live with having learned from my previous experiences of not having a job lined up upon graduation from my undergraduate degree years earlier. I was hired into the bank by a senior executive who at one time in his own career had responsibility for Aboriginal banking in Canada, so he appreciated and valued the experience and breadth of perspective I gained while in the Arctic Circle on my MBA consulting course assignment. Never would I have thought that such an obscure student experience could be a major factor in landing my first real career opportunity and start me on my path of professional life.

Over the course of the next few years, I worked hard and established a good track record in the process, securing progressively senior roles in the areas of retail banking strategy, operational risk management, global banking payments, and electronic banking. It was then that I had my first negative work experience as I had a line manager who, in my opinion, felt very threatened by me. It was not a pleasant environment to work in nor conducive to my productivity, mental well-being, and ongoing success. He continuously tried to block my exposure from senior executives and stifle anything that drew positive attention to my profile and professional accomplishments. Over time this environment became worse, and the negative environment led me to question the role I was in as something did not seem to fit well with me at the time … something about what I was doing and how I had to work did not feel right.

As it happened, the year was 2001 and as summer that year came to an end, the world was jolted by the horrible events of September 11, 2001—the terrorist attack in New York City that resulted in the destruction of the twin towers of the World Trade Center and the death of thousands of innocent lives. I remember the moment I saw the "Breaking News" bulletin on the news monitor in our office. I, like many others I imagine, could not believe what I was seeing; and for that moment in time, I felt the shock and horror of the event as though I was myself an American. I think for a moment in time that day, people all around the world stood in solidarity with the United States and Americans everywhere, just as I did.

A couple of months later as the aftermath of the attack started to take its toll on many financial institutions and economies worldwide, there was a huge string of job losses at my organization. I remember seeing the vice president of my department having to have meetings with people he did not even know and give them the bad news that they were being let go as there were just not enough senior managers to cover all the employees who were losing their jobs. By virtue of having my MBA, I was told by my own manager that my job was safe "for now," but I would probably lose my job during the next wave of job losses. I was asked to just find odd jobs to do until then to look busy.

This news was both jolting and unnerving. I'm not the kind of person who can sit around and twiddle my thumbs doing work that lacked purpose and meaning. I went home that day feeling sick to my stomach at what was inevitably going to happen. I went into work every day for the rest of the week just trying to get through the days with the feeling of nausea that persisted. I couldn't sleep properly and everything in my gut was telling me I had to get out of there. In some ways, the week was an important one in my life to help raise my self-awareness and respond to my feelings. This is another element of living a leadership lifestyle, which will be detailed more in Insight 2 later in this book.

On the last day of that week, I made a bold and risky decision and resigned without knowing what the future would hold. It just did not seem right staying there in light of the circumstances and I listened to my inner voice that was encouraging me to break loose from this situation on my own terms. Trusting your own feelings and listening to your inner voice is essential for living a leadership lifestyle and more can be found on this topic in Insight 4. Besides, I quite fancied going back to school to complete my doctorate degree. Lo and behold, that never happened. In fact, that idea never even got off the ground.

Several weeks passed and the gravity of what I had done finally caught up with me. What the heck did I just do to myself?! Here I am with no job, no income, and no sense of direction about what my next step was going to be. I was scared … no *terrified* is probably a more accurate description, and I had no one to blame but myself. Finding myself without a job or any prospects, and knowing that I was responsible for the situation, was one of the most humbling and stressful times in my life. Yet although it was quite difficult, I looked hard for the silver lining in the situation and soon found it after a period of deep reflection and acceptance.

I had frequently engaged in volunteer work since being in high school, so I thought I'd get involved in a good cause again as a way to constructively pass some of the time while I searched for a new role. This would give me something positive to focus on while I did some networking, and it would stop me from eating everything in sight in the kitchen cupboards as I sat at home in a stressed and depressive state during some times and bored out of my wits during others. (Sadly, this is still a challenge in my life when I get stressed, but I'm working on it!) I tried to look for a cause that I felt passionate about but struggled with this. There was too much going on inside my mind and I must admit the fear did not seem to dissipate at all during that time.

I needed help and had finally mustered the courage to talk to someone about what was going on. I was fortunate to line up a meeting with a former professor of mine who taught marketing strategy in my MBA program and who also happened to have previously worked as a senior executive at the bank from which I resigned. He had moved on from the bank by that time and was doing some corporate sponsorship consulting work for the organization arranging the Pope's visit to Canada for a global youth conference being organized by the Vatican.

Before I knew it, I was recruited to be part of the national organizing team planning and delivering the event—World Youth Day 2002—which was the largest event in Canadian history up to that point in time. It was like putting on the Olympics with the added obligation to house and feed the young people attending the conference—"pilgrims" they were called. Because of my commercial background and experience, I was asked to work on the corporate sponsorship team to cover for another person who was going on maternity leave. Although this kind of work was the furthest thing from my mind in terms of what my next professional steps would be, I quickly realized that this would be an opportunity that comes along once in a lifetime for someone like me and an opportunity to also build my personal brand by having a new experience and doing very different kind of work than I had done before, so I accepted the post with a flexible mindset, trust and—if you'll pardon the religious connotation given the circumstances—faith that everything will work out as it should, believing and accepting that this is just the next steppingstone on my leadership journey. I had learned through my MBA days that building my personal brand would be an important element of being successful, so I embraced the opportunity out of both need as well as a willingness to grow and develop. More on building and protecting your personal brand will be discussed in Insight 3.

While in this role, I had the opportunity to travel to New York City with special permission to visit Ground Zero to participate in a memorial service on the site of the former World Trade Center along with law enforcement and fire protection workers in New York. It was an experience that silenced everyone present as we prayed together to show our respect for those who had lost their lives in such a terrible attack and to demonstrate that hope was still alive. I was also privileged at the end of that assignment to get to meet His Holiness, Pope John Paul II (now Saint John Paul II). Although he was not a saint during his lifetime, the experience was inspirational and moving, and will be cherished my whole life.

Continental Shift

Once World Youth Day had taken place in August 2002, the legal entity that was set up to deliver the event had to be wound down. Once again, I found myself without a job and a bit directionless.

One of the corporate sponsors I worked with had given me very positive and inspiring feedback and encouraged me to stay within the not-for-profit sector if possible. He introduced me to a well-known youth charity in the United Kingdom called the Duke of Edinburgh's Award— the namesake charity of His Royal Highness, Prince Philip, the husband of Her Majesty, Queen Elizabeth II. Having had such an interesting and adventurous career path so far, I did my due diligence and learned that I could get a special working visa from the British government to move to the United Kingdom and find employment without needing any company sponsorship. By this point in time, I was in my early 30s and too old for any youth visas or travel/work permits usually given to people under 25 years of age; however, I qualified for a new program the British government introduced called the Highly Skilled Migrant Program.

Being true to a personal promise I made to myself earlier in my youth to make the most out of life, I availed myself of the opportunity to move to England on my own in 2003. Just like my move to Japan after I completed my undergraduate studies and post graduate certificate years earlier, I did not know anyone at all in England, although at least this time I could speak the language so I thought to myself, "How hard could this move be?"

These words would come to haunt me within a few months of my arrival in the United Kingdom. Although I knew the language, unlike my move to Japan I had no job lined up but having corresponded with many companies after receiving my visa and even having a few meetings and in some cases, interviews, with potential hiring managers, I was told I was very marketable, and their organizations would definitely consider hiring me. Hearing this, I had a fairly high degree of confidence in my plan to move to England on my own and take up a new role after I got myself settled. So, I made the move to another continent with hope, ambition, and inspiration. Shortly after arriving in the United Kingdom in early 2003, the second Iraq War broke out and many organizations were in a holding pattern due to the resulting uncertainty of the troubles in the Middle East. I found myself in London, one of the most expensive cities in the world to live in, during a period when the currency exchange was not in my favor and with a very limited amount of savings to draw upon as I had been working in the not-for-profit sector prior to my move. Life was, shall we say, "character building" during that time and many of my friends back in Canada thought I was crazy to have made such a risky move. In actuality, I had prepared more than people realized by visualizing the life I wanted to go after, planning for how I could achieve it, and then I put my plan in action. This visualizing, planning, and acting is also a part of living a leadership lifestyle and will be explained in more detail in Insight 5. I had planned carefully, meeting with a number of potential employers on a number of trips to London during the previous year. All indications led me to believe that I would have a very good chance of getting a job once I arrived. I could not have anticipated that war would break out.

This new development, however, taught me the importance of having a contingency plan. I explored every suitable opportunity that I possibly could in order to find a job and after months of being unemployed, it became a matter of survival.

One job I pursued was for an interesting role at a prominent museum in London, where after an astounding round of interviews with roughly about 45 people, I was shortlisted as one of the final two candidates for the job. Unfortunately, the position was awarded to a more senior professional with a track record of success in the United Kingdom and experience as a managing director at a large tier-1 consulting firm. I was informed that I was the popular choice for the role, but the other candidate was the safer bet given the difference in our length of experience in the United Kingdom and our tenure of overall professional experience. I was devastated to have come so close, but as they say at the Oscars, it was an honor to be nominated. About a month or so after missing out on that role it was make-or-break time for me. I was down to my last £200 GBP in the bank. Filled with fear, but still focused on the vision of what I was trying to achieve, I kept a positive attitude and stayed calm, confident in my resourcefulness, and accepting that everything happens for a reason. I listened to my inner voice and trusted my instincts and within a week I was offered a short-term maternity cover for a position in the education sector in the United Kingdom. After demonstrating my value to the organization during the following months, I was asked to apply for a more senior, permanent role when the maternity cover was finished. I was unsuccessful but asked to stay on in a more junior capacity.

At this point, it would been easy to accept the offer, ensuring my financial stability, which by the way was still in a very tenuous state. However, the permanent position available to me at that point was more junior than the maternity cover I completed, and it would have been awkward to deal with the resulting human dynamics in the workplace, and to be completely honest, at the time it felt like a huge step backward for me. Despite the short-term financial benefits it offered, taking the job was not the right thing for me to do and my value system would not permit me to accept the role in these circumstances.

For me, when I know the easy path is not the right path, my conclusion is that I should go in a different direction, even if it means a somewhat riskier one. Although I hadn't yet secured anything, I trusted that everything would work out as it should—and it did. The experience also made me reflect on the risks I had taken in my life, and I had to come to terms with the fact that risk is a part of life. Sometime the risks we take will work out, and at other times they may not. But if we don't try, we will never know. It also made me understand the importance of taking risks and helped me to learn and to accept that risk is also part of living a leadership lifestyle, which will be expanded upon in Insight 6.

From Rags to Riches (Well ... Not Quite Yet). Next Stop: Buckingham Palace

Within a week of declining the offer, I received an offer of employment from the Duke of Edinburgh's Award—the organization that had first motivated me to relocate to England.

Although I had been considered for a permanent role, I was once again not successful due to my lack of UK experience; however, my background was looked upon positively and I was offered a contract role, which I accepted with genuine gratitude to work alongside the successful candidate. Whew ... what a relief! And further proving how right I was to not take the education sector role I had recently turned down, I had worked at the Duke of Edinburgh's Award for just about one month when it became clear that the person who was appointed to the permanent senior role I initially tried out for turned out to be the wrong fit for the organization and decided to leave the company. When she resigned, I was offered the permanent role of deputy fundraising director for the Duke of Edinburgh's Award and I graciously accepted the permanent position and celebrated modestly that evening with some new friends and my flat mates over a round of drinks at our favorite local pub. After all the hard work I had put in and the ups and downs on my journey so far, it was important for me to celebrate the little successes along the way in a proportional way to mark these important steppingstones on my life's path. It's important to celebrate the successes along the way when you live a leadership lifestyle to mark the important milestones you achieve and provide encouragement and motivation for the future. More on this is described in Insight 11.

Within seven months of arriving in a new country and having no network of support to begin with and no local market work experience, I found myself in a fairly senior role in a high-profile national charity in the United Kingdom with royal patronage. And because of the nature of the work my department did, and after rigorous security and background checks, I also found myself with my own pass to enter Buckingham Palace where we were invited occasionally to organize fund raising lunch events presided over by HRH, the late Prince Phillip, the Duke of Edinburgh at times, and at other times presided over by HRH, Prince Edward, the Earl of Wessex (who was recently bestowed with the new title of Duke of Edinburgh by King Charles III, after the passing of their father, Prince Phillip), who was a trustee of the charity and played an active role in its ongoing success. Whoever would have thought that my long and winding career path to date would bring me to Buckingham Palace! Definitely not me. All I could think about was how lucky I was and had an immense feeling of gratitude, pride, and dare I say relief for having taken the path that had become my life's journey so far.

After a few successful years in the role, I was recruited by another charity, the National Youth Theatre of Great Britain, for a more senior position as development director. This role offered me the opportunity for more strategic influence and accountability for generating revenue for another national youth charity in the United Kingdom. In addition, as a member of the executive committee I had an opportunity to shape the future of the organization and take it forward. I also had the pleasure of meeting some amazing A-list celebrities from film, stage, and television who were connected to the National Youth Theatre in some way in their youth. My life's path had taken such an amazing route all because I made a bold and risky decision to seize the day, take ownership and personal responsibility for my own success, resign from an unpleasant work environment and a job that I was going to lose anyway, and fulfill a promise to myself by making the most of the opportunities that come my way.

CHAPTER 2

The Winding Road of My Middle Career Years

From London to Monaco, Then Back Home to Toronto

After a couple of years working at the National Youth Theatre, a coincidental meeting with a former colleague from Canada, took my career full circle back into the banking world. I went to pitch a corporate sponsorship opportunity for the charity at a tier-1 private bank in London where I bumped into a colleague I worked with in Toronto after my MBA. He was interested in what I was doing and curious about my day-to-day activities. We met several times to discuss this, and I hadn't realized this at the time, but I was discretely being assessed for transferability of skills and the potential to succeed in a new intake program that was being introduced in the private bank where he worked.

After several meetings with him and his colleagues, who were seeking to learn more about me and get to know me better, and after several well-enjoyed pints to catch up on old times, I was offered a wealth management role managing some of the bank's key relationships with ultra-high-net-worth clients based out of their offices in the Mayfair district of London. Here again was another amazing opportunity in front of me and, after a great deal of reflection and soul searching about how to move forward and staying true to the promise I made myself, although it was a difficult decision to make to leave the not-for-profit sector, I decided to accept the position and make the move back to the commercial sector to further develop my own skills and capabilities as a leader.

From Disdain and Prejudice to a Dream Offer

My first year was very tough. My entry into a new commercial role from the not-for-profit sector was met with skepticism from my new colleagues who did not believe I "fit the mold" or had what it takes to be successful in "their world." I was also met with a fair degree of prejudice and racism. Dealing with racism was not new for me, having grown up with this all my life because of my heritage. What was new to me this time, however, was the social, class-based prejudice common in the United Kingdom, and based on the fact that I did not study at Oxford or Cambridge and did not have a wealthy family background as many of my colleagues did in the wealth management office where I worked. I was once even told by a team leader of mine that he thought I would feel more comfortable in a different division of the bank based at a different location, because the staff there dealt with clients of a lower wealth level, and he thought I would fit in better there instead of the wealth management office where we were based dealing with the ultrahigh-net-worth client segment, the wealthiest clients of the private bank.

I guess I had started to develop a tougher skin by that point in my life as I never let those comments nor the prejudice and racism I faced bother me. Faced with this new adversity in my work environment, I was determined to prove my critics wrong, thinking back to all the times in my past I'd had to overcome challenges put in front of me. My colleagues barely made any effort to get to know me and showed very little, if any, support. I was constantly being judged and every action I took was closely scrutinized by others in the workplace. There seemed to be an office culture of "everyone out for themselves"—affirming the myth of corporate jobs in the financial sector.

Nevertheless, I worked hard and stayed focused on my vision for success, trusting in my ability, ambition, personal resourcefulness, and desire to succeed no matter what challenges I faced, and knowing deep down what I was truly capable of, if I just put my mind to it and applied myself. I strengthened my resolve to succeed and persistently worked hard, confident in the leadership skills I had already developed. The failures I had experienced in the past proved to be positive for me as they not only helped me learn how to avoid making some mistakes, but also helped me better understand my own strengths and weaknesses and to have confidence and trust in myself knowing that I was continuing to build and develop my resilience to bounce back from difficult situations. Building your resilience is important for living a leadership lifestyle and this will be discussed further in Insight 7.

As a result of all my hard work and focus, I had an impressive first year with results exceeding many experienced and tenured colleagues. This success seemed to have gotten me noticed and I was asked if I'd be interested in relocating to Monaco to help the business there to grow. Could this really be happening? Monaco? Land of the uber-wealthy and the Monaco Grand Prix in the famed city of Monte Carlo? Subject of one of the first Disney movies I saw in Canada when my family just immigrated there, Herbie goes to Monte Carlo—a nostalgic family classic still enjoyed today! And, of course, setting for many a scene in the infamous James Bond (aka 007) movies.

I recalled backpacking through Europe during the summer before my final year of my Bachelor degree. I was about 19 years old when I first traveled to Monaco (in student style just to be clear) and I clearly remember standing at a scenic spot in front of the Palace, looking down on a small marina in town and saying quietly to myself, "One day I'm going to live here." Seventeen years had passed since that backpacking holiday, and suddenly the opportunity to live there was presenting itself. This truly was a dream come true. How many people in the world have the chance to actually realize one of their life's dreams? It was an opportunity too good to pass up and as it was for the same company I was already working for, there was very little negative impact on my professional life.

Having done some preliminary due diligence on the place to mitigate my risks and being open to new experiences to continue this path of lifelong learning and personal growth and development that I once realized I was traveling, I decided to take a calculated risk, yet again, and accepted the role. The decision came with a hefty personal cost: I was just getting settled in my life in the United Kingdom, I was starting to establish good social networks as well as helpful support systems, so uprooting myself again and starting over was not only daunting but also inconvenient at this point in my life. But my gut instinct told me that the experience would further help me learn and grow, and so despite the negatives I was aware of, I jumped at the chance to continue my quest for professional and personal leadership development and growth.

I was relocated to Monaco by my company at the end of August 2008. The great part was that as this was a company relocation, all my relocation expenses were paid for, and I even received a very generous allowance to get me set up in the new place. I also had my choice of company car; since I was now living on the Riviera, I selected a new BMW convertible of course (which I looked amazing in if I do say so myself). This dream just seemed to be getting better and better. Here I was, starting all over again in yet another new place and another language (the working language was French this time) in which I had only elementary skills having studied French in primary school and high school. But after a few years of hard work and perseverance, I seemed to have "arrived" and what a great feeling it was.

The Dream Crashes but Eventually Recovers

I mentioned my relocation was at the end of August 2008. For me, that time will always be remembered as the time I moved to Monaco. For most other people, however, that time will be forever remembered as the time when the global credit crisis of 2008 hit and financially impacted so many companies and people around the world.

Contrary to all my expectations and hopes, my first year in Monaco would prove to be filled with challenge, difficulty, and profound unhappiness. I did not have the same kind of success as I had in London and once again, I felt that I was under the microscope. I had significant difficulty bringing on new business, and there were rumors that my job might be at risk because the credit crisis was taking its toll on every company. I seemed to be sinking deeper and deeper into a hole and it was a very uncomfortable feeling for me, and a time filled with a great deal of fear. Being new in the place and so far away from family and friends, my unhappiness was compounded by feelings of isolation and loneliness. Looking back now, I realize I was probably sinking into some sort of depression. The expectations and fantasy I had of this amazing relocation did not align with my reality. Even though having all the bells and whistles such as the

BMW convertible made things a bit easier, I realized what I had always known—that material things can bring you comfort, but never really bring you happiness.

The combination of the global financial environment and my poor work performance led me to a depressive state that was hard to shake. I even learned that I was going to be put on a performance improvement program at work. This is a kind of support program for nonperformers to help them improve their results—but which often became a preamble to them losing their jobs. I was in a state of shock, finding it difficult to accept that I had been put on a performance improvement program! I'd had to deal with setbacks in life before but never like this. It was much more public and very embarrassing and the stress I was dealing with became almost intolerable.

To add insult to injury, that year I was awarded only 1-Euro for my annual bonus and everyone on my team was aware of it. I can't say for certain, but it may be that my manager was forced to enter something into the compensation system and hence the 1-Euro. If it were possible, he may have entered 0 … and to be honest, I'm not sure which of the two is worse. It was like getting a proverbial slap in the face. I was mortified and embarrassed beyond belief. I was also angry and just wanted to lash out at the world.

Keeping true to my personal values and the personal brand I had built and established throughout my career, however, I held my tongue and once again did some deep soul searching and reflection. Should I quit because of the way I'd been treated? I was certainly ready to do this. But I didn't want to act hastily when I was in such an emotional state and so far away and isolated from any personal support system. And through my reflection I came to accept that I did have a role in this situation as it was my poor performance that resulted in my ending up in this position, even though market dynamics globally were quite difficult at the time. It was important to me to make a considered decision for my next step and to make sure I had thought through the consequences.

My inner voice and gut instincts were like a moral compass for me during that time. Was I going to let this latest setback in my life—albeit one that seemed to me to be the biggest one yet—rob me of the amazing opportunity I was having to live one of my dreams by being in Monaco? Absolutely not! I gave myself permission to be upset. I gave myself permission to be disappointed. I gave myself permission to be humbled by the whole experience and I gave myself permission to accept this failure of mine and learn from this whole negative experience. I chose to put my pride aside and be open to the support, encouragement, and coaching the company was going to provide. After all, although the company was not obligated, it was willing to try and help me if I chose to accept the help it was offering. After a few days of emotional ups and downs, I was ready to move forward and accepted the offer for the company support through the performance improvement program.

I hadn't realized this at the time because I was so blinded by my own arrogance and self-pity, that all my teammates were rooting for me and were happy I chose to stick it out to try and improve my performance. Many of them told me that taking ownership of my situation, accepting what was happening, and trying to do something constructive to make the situation better and not just complaining about it was a testament to my true character. I was humbled and grateful for their supportive and encouraging words. There I was thinking that nobody was supporting me, and the truth is that I had many supporters ... albeit silent ones. I learned that I should not be so quick to judge, and to understand that every person is different and reacts differently to different situations.

Many of my colleagues also shared with me privately that they themselves were on performance improvement programs at one time or another in their careers and suddenly I no longer felt so embarrassed or alone. Through discussions with colleagues during that period, I also learned that I should judge myself by more than just my performance in my job and that's a lesson I've actively applied in my life ever since. After three months on the performance improvement program, I had regained my momentum and once again felt gratitude for all that I have been through and the person I had become. I had experienced failure for reasons both within and out of my control, but regardless of the cause or whose fault it was, it was up to me to bounce back and pull myself out of a slump with the help and support of some teammates. The icing on the cake for me was winning the company chairman's award both in 2009 for my individual contribution to the company and again in 2011 for my contribution to the region I worked in. After a little while and more reflection, I realized that what I thought of as a monumental failure was just another opportunity in disguise. This mindset of reframing failure as an opportunity will be expanded upon later in the book in Insight 8.

Homeward Bound

After several years in that company, I felt the need to spread my wings and join a new company to continue my growth and development and later that year joined another company in Monaco. After three months at the new firm, I was let go, along with seven other new employees who had all started at the same time as me. The company had hired a new group chief executive who had made some strategic changes in light of changing regulatory frameworks around the world. Please, someone, tell me how to get off this roller-coaster! I had taken calculated risks in life before, but this time the risk had not worked out as I had hoped.

Around the same time that all the drama with the new company was occurring, I was confronted with the news that my mother and stepfather were not in the best of health. Through all my travels and adventures internationally, I guess I lost track of time and hadn't realized that so many years had passed. Even though I'd gone back to Toronto for holidays and special family occasions, I hadn't been around to see my parents aging. It was getting more difficult for my parents to move around, and both my mother and stepfather had to undergo some surgery in the coming months. As I was alone and at that point unemployed in Monaco, I did some soul searching and having time on my hands and a little bit of money saved up, I decided to stay for a whole month in Toronto when I returned for the Christmas holidays. I'd never before been able to take so much vacation time, so it was the perfect opportunity to spend some time with my family. And I think with everything that had gone on in my career and life so far, coupled with a feeling of profound despair and uncertainty, I probably needed to go home again and experience the feeling of unconditional love that only family can provide. I went back to Toronto that December and absolutely loved being back. It was exactly the kind of safe and secure retreat I needed at the time. I found myself once again worried about what the future would bring, but at least this time I could feel my fear lessen with the comfort of some of my mother's and sister's home cooking. There's nothing like home cooking to comfort you. And, yes, the usual sounds of family arguments over the most mundane of things were also welcome distractions during that time in my life.

As it was the holiday season, when I was able to I tried to catch up with old friends, past colleagues, and even mentors with whom I had lost touch. It was just the tonic I needed to recharge my batteries. One of my life mentors from well over 10 years back suggested I think hard about moving back to Canada permanently as all my international experience would be highly valued in Toronto. Not many people had the life and professional path that I had, he explained. He even opened the door to a possible employment opportunity by sending an e-mail to one of his contacts.

Before I knew it, I was interviewing for a high-profile senior role at another large Canadian financial institution. This wasn't the intended purpose of my return to Toronto, but I realized then that sometimes life takes you to exactly where you need to be, when you need to be there—and not knowing your future direction does not mean you don't have one. Yes, those were uncomfortable and uncertain times, but dealing with all the ambiguity that was in my life at that moment was also teaching me valuable lessons and building my leadership character.

Before my month in Toronto was over, and even though it was the Christmas period and not much usually happens employment-wise during holiday time, I was fortunate to be offered a high-profile wealth management leadership position. It was a sales leadership position: I would be leading the top team of private bankers at the flagship office of one of Canada's largest and most successful banks. Excited at the new direction my career was taking, I moved back to Toronto a couple of months later to commence the new role with enthusiasm and excitement.

Although I was new to the general management responsibilities of the business, I embraced all the ups and downs that came along with the role. I knew that I would make mistakes, after all I'm human, and because of the high-profile nature of the role, I also knew that I would again be under scrutiny from many different people. I tried to succeed in every way I could. I tried to be resourceful in every way I could. I stayed open to all the coaching and support the company would give me. I pushed aside my pride and asked for help whenever I needed. And I tried, more than anything else, to stay true to my values and to be an authentic leader embracing my own personal brand. It was the only way I knew how to lead—simply by being myself, and also being true to myself, which might resonate with some people, and perhaps not with others. What was most important was to stay focused on our goals and treat everyone with respect. As a leader, I knew I was a role model to others and I realized then the importance of living a life—regardless of whether a personal or professional context—with integrity, compassion, and being true to your values.

The first year in the role was, as you can imagine, challenging to say the least. There was so much to learn, so much change in my life coming at me all at once, and so many mistakes to make. You guessed it, I made all those mistakes and probably even more that I haven't realized. But I learned from them as quickly as I could and never made those mistakes again … at least I hope I didn't.

Year two went much better and I had quickly established my personal leadership brand within the organization. At the end of my second year, and then again at the end of my third year, I was simultaneously privileged and humbled to have won awards for being one of the top sales leaders for the business across the country, measured against key performance indicators and success criteria and ranked alongside my peers on a league table. Winning once is an accomplishment in itself, but two years in a row … that was meaningful to me. The credit of course was not mine to enjoy alone. I only won because of the incredible teamwork and dedication of every member of the team I was privileged to lead. I was making my mark in this new company and more importantly, I felt like I was contributing to the success of the business and the team. But something kept niggling at my insides that made it difficult for me to feel settled.

Successful, yet Unfulfilled

After three successful years in Toronto, I finally admitted to myself that I wasn't feeling quite fulfilled with what I was doing. I was grateful that my parents' health issues had recovered, but there was something missing in my life: a clarity of purpose that aligned with my personal value system and innermost passion. Although I'd had what many would consider the good fortune to have opportunities to live and work all around the world,

I felt that there was a hidden calling in life that needed to be explored further. I wasn't quite sure what that next step was, but I knew it involved helping other people to succeed and overcome the challenges they faced when trying to achieve their goals.

Coupled with this, I realized that all the moving around I did in my life to pursue my career and life dreams had left me feeling that I didn't know where "home" was anymore. Even though I was raised in Toronto and family members were (and still are) living there, it no longer felt like home to me. Sure, it was easy for me to fit in no matter where I went, but not feeling the emotional connection of "home" left me wanting. Time for more soul searching and reflection. Time to decide whether it would be suitable or not to take another calculated risk in life. Time for my personal leadership journey to continue once more. Time, once again, to confront the uncertainty of my future to avoid stagnation and life stalling. I had to once again be courageous and carve my own path and more is written about this element of living a leadership lifestyle in Insight 9.

I thought very carefully about my next steps, this time consciously telling myself that I was ready to plant my roots somewhere for the long term. After a period of deep contemplation and self-reflection that lasted a number of months, as well as consultation with my closest circle of trusted friends and family members—those who knew me well and always supported me through the ups and downs that life put in my path—I decided it was time to move back to London and very consciously make a home for myself. Through all my career travels and amazing life experiences, London was the place I most felt at home. I was going to trust that instinct, believe in my own abilities, and take personal accountability for my own destiny, even though that destiny may be filled with fear, excitement, anticipation, happiness, and clarity of purpose. I was just going to go for it one way or another. I made a conscious choice to continue to move forward in the direction of my dreams, this time with a clarity of purpose unlike any I had known before.

Armed with this new-found clarity, I started to think about all the life lessons I had learned along the way and then started to plan my next step, trying to incorporate everything I had learned through my life's path to date.

CHAPTER 3

London Calling

The Wonder Years Begin

Before relocating back to the United Kingdom, I planned for about four or five months, exercising patience, and trying to be as strategic as possible to mitigate any risks that might accompany this next move. I reviewed my finances and made sure I had a sufficient financial cushion to carry me through the initial period of uncertainty. I reconnected with past friends and professional contacts to help ease my social transition back into London life. And I made sure to continue to focus on the future and all that was possible, rather than look backward and dwell on the past. More importantly, after all the life experience I had gained so far, I decided that I was going to define what progress and success would look like and meant for me with these next steps I'm taking, very conscious of the fact that there were bound to be ups and downs on the road ahead. Having your own definition of progress and success is an important element of living a leadership lifestyle, which is the topic of focus in Insight 10.

I arrived back in the United Kingdom in the summer of 2015. This time around, I knew a bit more of what to expect from London life. Although many past friends and professional contacts have moved on, I was excited about all the new and interesting people I was going to meet in this next chapter of my life. And I was excited about all the new and interesting things I was going to learn through the next stage of my lifelong learning by being, well I suppose I have to face it by now, a kind of student of life and a student for life, thinking about all new possibilities for growth I had yet to learn and experience. Insight 12 expands on the mindset of lifelong learning for living a leadership lifestyle.

Once again, there was no job lined up, so I took myself out of my comfort zone and decided to be a type of social entrepreneur. I set up my own business offering leadership coaching and consulting for professionals in large and small companies, entrepreneurs setting up shop for themselves, emerging leaders new to leadership roles within their organizations or new to people management, and private clients personally motivated to invest in developing their leadership skills and capabilities.

A Path to Success and Happiness by Living a Leadership Lifestyle

Through all my amazing personal and professional experiences in life, I've come to realize that to be happy and successful in life takes much more than professional accomplishments. At times this will require you to make some difficult choices to achieve your objectives, but it will be worthwhile. Making hard choices is essential for living a leadership lifestyle and more is written about that in Insight 13.

Success and happiness require leading a leadership lifestyle every day and in every facet of your life, professional and personal. You have to be self-aware; you have to trust your instincts and listen to your inner voice; you have to make different and at many times difficult choices that may be challenging in the short term but beneficial in the longer term, and you have to take time to celebrate little successes along the way. You have to take risks that may or may not work out; you have to work hard, stay focused on the vision for your future, your plan to achieve your goals, and take action to achieve your objectives. You have to be persistent to develop your resilience and both recognize and accept that progress is not always linear. You have to be open to lifelong learning and be flexible when called upon, especially in situations of great ambiguity and uncertainty. And you have to be true to yourself and your values; and put in the hard work when needed to go after your dreams while maintaining a lifelong learning mindset to see the varied opportunities that cross your path as you live your own leadership lifestyle.

In Part 2 of this book, I share with you these and other key leadership lifestyle insights I learned along the way, as well as offer you some simple and easy leadership lifestyle exercises I created for you to complete, which I regularly used for myself as I emerged as a leader and continue to live my own leadership lifestyle even today.

The 13 insights are as follows:

1. You are accountable for your own success.
2. Be self-aware and respond to your feelings.
3. Build and protect your personal brand.
4. Trust your instincts. Listen to your inner voice.
5. Visualize. Plan. Act.
6. Accept that risk is part of a leadership lifestyle.
7. Build your persistence.
8. Failure is just opportunity in disguise.
9. Be courageous and carve your own path.
10. You define progress and success.
11. Celebrate the successes along the way.
12. Be a student of life, and a student for life.
13. Make the difficult choices that are needed.

I am passionate about helping others to succeed and realize their leadership potential and it brings me great joy if, by living your own leadership lifestyle, you pursue your hopes and dreams the leadership lifestyle way and achieve success in the process.

PART 2

Insights for Living a Leadership Lifestyle

INSIGHT 1

You Are Accountable for Your Own Success

You—and only you—have the ultimate power to shape your world and take control of your own success. It's very easy to make up excuses for why things may not be the way you want them to be. This mindset—the victim mindset—is a self-perpetuating killer of dreams that operates in a vicious circle and downward spiral. A victim mentality occurs when a person feels they are the victim of negative circumstances or the actions of others, and as a result, they develop a negative outlook on life. Because they don't think anything is their fault, they don't take any responsibility for what happens to themselves in life … they just let life happen to them. Early in life, I heard someone say something that has stayed with me ever since: "If you take responsibility for your life, you will take control of your life." If you remember these words and apply them in your life, then you'll never have to worry about the victim mindset again.

Make Time to Develop Yourself

In the world of sports, athletes don't expect to be successful unless they train for athletic success. They dedicate a significant amount of time and energy to improving and enhancing their performance, and this improve-ment comes over time, not as a spontaneous burst. Famed footballer Cristiano Ronaldo's work ethic is legendary. He is one of the world's best because he continuously pushes himself and continuously strives to make himself better. To observers, success may seem to come very easily. Only the athletes in training know how much hard work they have to put in to further develop their skills; only they know the investment they have to make in themselves for this growth and development to occur and for the improvement and success to come. And the truly wise athletes know that success is always the result of a number of factors, including disci-pline, training, coaching, compromise, and support from others who are cheering them on.

The most successful people in the world are those who never stop trying to get better, even when they reach the highest levels of their professions. Professional golfers who have won major golf tournaments (and become multimillionaires in the process) still work with coaches. Throughout his career—even into his 80s—famous cellist Pablo Casals always gave the same answer when asked why he still practices for hours every day: "Because I'm making progress."

If we know from the previous examples of athletes and musicians in "training" that developing oneself is a key element in achieving success, why, then, are so many people skeptical or reluctant to invest time in improving themselves beyond their formal education years? Do people secretly *not* want to succeed? Or is it that they think they have already learned what they need in order to achieve continued success with any chosen goal?

You can never invest enough in your own personal development and success. Successful leaders are open-minded to invest in their own suc-cess, embarking on a journey of lifelong learning for personal develop-ment. At many different points in my career, I tried to find opportunities to invest in personal development. When I first started working in the financial sector, I sought out opportunities to learn new skills by asking my manager for specific training so that I could develop beyond what was required. I remember specifically asking to go on time management courses offered to employees in the company because my role involved juggling many different streams of work and it was sometimes difficult to stay on top of things. I had a supportive manager who was eager to help me develop professionally, and so he authorized training whenever I asked for it, as most of my peers usually rolled their eyes whenever work training was mentioned in the workplace. I started with the time management course and then asked to go on a number of other training courses to become more proficient with computer software applications, organizational skills, delivering effective presentations, and running successful meetings. I also asked to go on any communications-related courses I could find to help with both my spoken and written communication skills, as it became apparent to me very quickly once I started working that providing clarity throughout your communications helps accelerate achievement of work goals, especially when others are involved and necessary to help you achieve your objectives. As a result, not only did I get some good skills training early on in my career for skills that I would continue to use through my lifetime, but I also got some great exposure to new areas of the company and got to establish some wonderful relationships with colleagues who worked in other parts of the organization whom I would most likely never come across through my daily work. This enabled me to learn about other parts of the company, get exposure, and become more knowledgeable about other workstreams within the company, which served to increase the value I was able to add through my own work by factoring in any impact on other parts of the organization beyond just my own team and functional area. And it made my own manager look good in front of his peers, so he was very happy to let me continue to go on training programs whenever he could. Often, taking these training programs meant having to put in some extra hours as well as take on extra work. But in the end, it was worth it as it enabled me to differentiate myself from other co-workers, develop new skills, and establish new relationships that would serve me well in the future. At several points in my life, I even chose to continue my education in a more formal capacity. After I completed my MBA, there was a long period of professional activity; but after a couple of decades of working, however, I realized I needed to update my skills and went back to school to pursue further qualifications more relevant to the work I was doing at the time.

This choice posed many challenges, but the struggles I faced helped me to grow and develop even further, and when I look back at the benefits that investing in myself had brought, I have no doubt whatsoever that it was the right decision. In fact, it was such a valuable experience that even after finishing that program, I decided to carry on my lifelong learning yet again, which is teaching me new skills and opening new doors in both my professional and personal lives that would not have been possible before.

Look After Your Health and Well-Being

Investing in your personal development can take many forms and doesn't always involve education or formal training. In order to be the best "you" possible, you have to nurture *all aspects* of your life, so they develop in a well-rounded way. Engaging in regular physical activity helps nurture the body. Making time daily or weekly for a period of reflection or meditation can help clear the mind and relieve stress. Actively learning something new helps to keep your mind sharp. Cooking a healthy meal can be both therapeutic and nutritionally beneficial. Spending quality time with family and friends can be uplifting. Make sure to look at and think of your "self" as a complete whole and try not to nurture one side of yourself at the expense of another. Try to nurture all sides of yourself in as balanced a way as possible.

Many years ago, when I was working in a risk management business within a large bank in Toronto, a valued mentor of mine (his name is Tony), who has since become a close friend and confidante, shared with me a model he often used to help him keep a healthy perspective on life. He suggested our lives could be viewed as an equilateral triangle, with all sides of the triangle being the same length and all internal angles being 60 degrees. One tip of the triangle represented our *health and well-being*. Another tip of the triangle represented our *public and professional selves*. And the third tip of the triangle represented our *personal and private lives*. The challenge in life was to maintain a balance among all three of these aspects so that the lengths and angles stayed the same. If any one aspect was suffering, one of the angles would shift, and the triangle, no longer equilateral, would be tilted and misshaped. To get to a positive place again, the task was to take some form of action targeting the tip that was off kilter to get the triangle to become equilateral again. I still employ this model today and use it as an internal measure to gauge how balanced my life is instead of making excuses for why something is going wrong or why I'm not achieving the results I want.

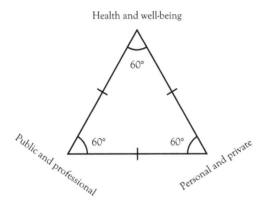

Equilateral triangle model for a balanced life

At one point later in my life, I found myself in a situation where the personal side of my life was very off-kilter, despite things seeming to be great on the surface. I had the good fortune of working abroad in one of the most beautiful places I've ever traveled to. I was transferred from London, UK, to Monte Carlo, Monaco, along the French Riviera to take up a new role at my company's local business in that region. At first, I was so happy … it was like a dream come true to be living and working in such a beautiful place. But a few months after relocating there, reality started to set in. The impact of the relocation was negative in ways I had never anticipated, and I found myself very lonely and unhappy despite all the good things I had going for me. Although the place seemed beautiful and ideal, I found it hard to meet like-minded people with the same interests and outlook on life that I had, and as a result, it was hard to establish good friendships and relationships. I realized that my personal life circumstances were very different from most people living in the area, and this just made it more difficult to connect with people in a meaningful way. When I think back on that time, I often think that the good fortune of having that experience just happened 10 years too early in my life. I was very unhappy and lonely, and this started to permeate all aspects of my life. When I started to have difficult challenges in my work life as a result of this, I just sank into a very dark hole at that point in time. As humans, we sometimes sink into moments of sadness, denial, and even depression. There may be elements of ourselves that we do not like, so we consciously or unconsciously employ defense mechanisms to cope. For example, we try to mask the things we don't like by neglecting them altogether or pretending that they do not exist. We try to convince ourselves that if we don't acknowledge these things, they will just go away or disappear on their own. We try to talk ourselves into thinking the situation is better than it really is because we are afraid to admit the truth. When we do these things, we are just fooling ourselves, but the sad part is that we are causing self-harm in the process. It's only by confronting and accepting our circumstances that we start to understand what we need to do and how to live our daily lives to achieve the kind of success and fulfilment we crave.

The personal side of my own life's equilateral triangle was horribly off-kilter, so I had to take some action to rebalance it. When the time was right, I was able to get myself out of that hole by making the very difficult decision to leave and move somewhere I thought I would be happier and where I would thrive rather than accepting a situation that made me unhappy and left me unfulfilled. By doing this, I was able to rebalance my own equilateral life triangle and get myself back on track. I realized that I was accountable for my own success, and I did something about it.

Believe in Yourself

For the spiritual among us, there is a great need and comfort in believing in something bigger, unexplainable, and more powerful than ourselves. Often, people believe in a deity or force of some sort that cannot be seen, heard, or felt, but there is great certainty that it exists. I suppose you can call this faith. While many people believe in something greater than themselves, they struggle to believe in their own ability to achieve success. By this, I'm not referring to an arrogant or unrealistic belief that you will always achieve everything you set your mind to accomplish regardless of the reality of the situation, but a genuine belief that with a positive attitude and a bit of focused work and patience, you will develop and progress at whatever you set your mind to, and achievement will be inevitable. In order to succeed, you must genuinely believe that you *can* and *will* succeed, and once you've found this belief, you must never let it go.

Believing in yourself is vitally important to achieving your goals. People are constantly bombarded with messages of negativity that lead to insecurity and fear. How many times have you had a great idea, perhaps one that is a little bit out of the ordinary or something that has never been done before, and you're told by others that it will be impossible to achieve? What's worse, how many times have you talked yourself out of even attempting to achieve a goal or make a dream come true because you're full of self-doubt and perhaps fear that you will not succeed? It isn't fair to expect success if you yourself don't even believe that it can be achieved.

A long time ago, I saw a great job being advertised that I really wanted and decided to apply. It was a relationship management role within an international banking electronic payments business. I would have to manage a portfolio of institutional clients made up of tier 2 and 3 banks located in Europe, the Middle East, and Africa. The primary task of my role was to monitor and manage the volume of business our banks would be doing with each other and grow those volumes over time. In short, it was a kind of sales role, but on an international level with significant responsibility. It would mean I got to travel internationally periodically to meet with my clients, and this was one of the main perks to me at the time (although the reality of having to travel to 10 different cities in 10 days on one business trip would soon lose its luster as I had the rudest of awakenings about what international business travel is all about). But it was cool for someone my age (I think I was about 27 at the time) to get such a role with such a level of responsibility ... I was considered a bit young for the role, so I needed to prove that I could do it. Although I did not meet all the requirements they were looking for, including the length of work experience, I met some of the requirements, and I believed in my ability to learn quickly and develop into the role. I shared my interest in the role with some of my colleagues and work contemporaries, whom I thought would show support and encourage me to help overcome any lingering self-doubt that had built up inside me; however, I was surprised—and not in a good way—when they tried to talk me out of it. This role was perfect for me, but I realized that these co-workers had not seen the different sides of me that I knew would make me successful in the role, so I had to rely on my own self-belief to cope with and overcome my doubts. When I got the call to interview, I was excited and started preparing for the meeting well in advance. I anticipated tricky interview questions, including those that may challenge the fact that I didn't meet all the requirements being asked for, and prepared considered responses to remove any doubts that the interviewers may have in my abilities. When the time came for the interview, I felt calm and on top of the situation, taking comfort in the fact that I had done all I could to maximize my chances of success. The interview went great, and I was ecstatic when I was informed that I got the job. When I asked for feedback from the hiring manager, I was told that it was my preparation and positive attitude that put me over the top. Although other candidates had all the technical skills required and more work experience, it was my energy and my ability to face a challenging situation head-on and give it my all that made me stand out. The manager felt that the technical skills required could be easily and quickly learned by someone like me who demonstrated an open mind and eagerness to learn along with my drive, positive attitude, and enthusiastic energy.

I don't want to make it sound like believing in yourself will always end up with the result you want. Indeed, there were many, many occasions when my belief in myself and my abilities did not work out the way I hoped. But despite those many setbacks, I tried not to let the negative outcome result in more self-doubt. I asked for feedback so I could better understand what happened and learn what I could have done differently or better; I then applied that learning the next time around. More importantly, I tried not to let myself slip into the victim mindset and get angry at others nor at myself. I took time to accept what had happened and to reflect on the circumstances I was in. And I continued to believe in myself and have faith that if I continued to work hard and try my best, eventually things would work out. And they did!

I've known many colleagues who were afraid to put their name forward and always talked themselves out of even applying for the job they wanted, thinking it was beyond them. Rather than expending energy talking themselves out of trying, they should have spent that energy finding reasons why they were the right person for the job and devising a plan to fill any competency gaps once in the role. There will always be naysayers who enjoy telling you why you can't or shouldn't do something. When you come across these people, listen politely to what they have to say and be open to their input and feedback, but don't let them convince you of something without properly reflecting on their words and believing in yourself. More often than not, those who enjoy giving you all the negatives are afraid themselves; without the courage to take the steps you want to take, they will hold you back. In some instances, they are also jealous of you for even considering some of the daring choices you may want to make because they know that they could never make the same choices themselves. Believing in yourself genuinely and wholeheartedly without arrogance or conceit is critical for you to move forward in life and achieve your goals.

A Lesson in Resilience

I've worked with people who refused to believe in themselves, even though they had everything going for them. They were healthy, able-bodied, capable, and attractive. They had no financial difficulties. They had a strong family foundation and a great deal of support from friends and loved ones. Yet they were never able to break free of the self-imposed barriers they had, the greatest ones being their lack of self-confidence and the willingness and courage to try.

I've also worked with others who have had to face nothing but adversity all their lives. They came from broken homes, experienced a great deal of financial difficulty throughout their lives, and have had to deal with serious health problems. Yet their positive attitude, their belief and faith in themselves, and their ability to overcome the challenges they faced kept them going no matter what or how many hardships they faced. Their *resilience quotient* was continually being tested, and each successive test was being passed with flying colors, as they were constantly reinforcing the message to themselves that they had the wherewithal to succeed simply by picking themselves up and trying again.

Many years ago, I worked with an amazing woman named Leah, who inspired me greatly with the many lessons I learned about resilience just from observing her from afar. She was a single mother of two, and one of her children was autistic. Life had dealt her many challenges, and her path was filled with many obstacles, both personal and financial. Maybe she did not see her situation this way, but in all honesty, I did because I'm not sure how I would have coped with the situations she had to deal with on a regular basis. Regardless of all the challenges she faced, however, she always tried to maintain her positive attitude and outlook on life, never giving up on her hopes and dreams for the future, both for herself and her family. More importantly, in all the years I worked with her, I don't ever recall a time where she stopped trying. And she was always available to help others whenever someone asked. I'm happy to say that our working relationship has since transformed into a lifelong friendship, and we still keep in touch regularly to this day, supporting and encouraging each other along our life paths whenever needed. Leah is someone I think of as a beacon of strength, courage, inspiration, self-belief, and positive energy, and she is one of the examples of success and leadership that I often speak about in a motivational and inspirational way when I'm coaching clients for their leadership development.

Embrace the Uncertainty

Martin Luther King once said, "Faith is taking the step even when you don't see the whole staircase." Believing in yourself may require you to admit that you don't have perfect knowledge and control of what is to come, and you may need to have a bit of faith that everything will work out as it should. If you lack belief in yourself, you may feel exposed to negative elements that hinder your success, or you may be vulnerable to outside influences slowing down your progress. Letting go and accepting what you don't know nor control is very difficult, even for the most successful of people. But with regular reflection and practice, you realize that developing the ability to believe in yourself, even with a great deal of uncertainty, can be an extremely liberating experience. By accepting what you can and cannot control, you begin to identify, acknowledge, focus on, and act on the things you can influence that can help you progress, and you don't waste time and energy on things beyond your control. By believing that you will succeed, your time will be used more effectively to propel you toward the achievement of your goals, and you won't get distracted by things that will slow you down, such as self-doubt, which can and will hinder your progress and success.

It truly is all about you. Take full control and ownership of your life and accept that your thoughts, actions, and attitude are the keys to unleashing your success. It's not just mind over matter: it's both mind *and* matter that are required. No more excuses … it's time to take that first step … it's time to move forward and try with the confidence and self-belief that you *can* and *will* achieve your goals step by step, and in the process, you will grow and develop yourself in ways you may never have previously imagined. Believe in yourself and your talents, and never give up hope that you can achieve what you set out to do.

Leadership Lifestyle Reflection: Dealing With Adversity

Parable of the Carrot, the Egg, and the Coffee
(Author Unknown)

A young woman went to her mother and told her how hard things were in her life. She did not know how she was going to make it and wanted to give up. She was tired of struggling. It seemed that after one problem was solved, a new one arose. Her mother took her to the kitchen. She filled three pots with water and placed each on a high fire.

Soon the pots came to a boil. In the first, she placed carrots; in the second, she placed eggs; and in the last, she placed ground coffee beans. She let them sit and boil without saying a word. In about 30 minutes, she turned off the burners. She fished the carrots out and placed them in a bowl. She pulled the eggs out and placed them in a bowl. Then she ladled the coffee out and placed it in a bowl.

Turning to her daughter, she asked, "Tell me, what you see?" "Carrots, eggs, and coffee," she replied. Her mother brought her closer and asked her to feel the carrots. She did and noted that they

---

(Continues)

(*Continued*)

were soft. The mother then asked the daughter to take an egg and break it. After pulling off the shell, she observed the hard-boiled egg. Finally, the mother asked the daughter to sip the coffee. The daughter smiled as she tasted its richness. The daughter then asked, "What does it mean, mother?"

Her mother explained that each of these objects had faced the same adversity ... boiling water. Each reacted differently. The carrot went in strong, hard, and unrelenting. However, after being subjected to the boiling water, it softened and became weak. The egg had been fragile. Its thin outer shell had protected its liquid interior, but after sitting through the boiling water, its interior hardened. The ground coffee beans were unique, however. After they were in the boiling water, they changed the water. "Which are you?" she asked her daughter. "When adversity knocks on your door, how do you respond? Are you a carrot, an egg, or a coffee bean?"

How about you? Does the boiling water of pain and setbacks change you? Have you gone into hardship fragile like an egg but come out hardened and bitter? Do you meet hardship head-on, strong like a carrot, only to be softened and defeated? Or, like the coffee beans, have you allowed the situation to be an opportunity for growth and change? Remember, you're accountable for your own success. No matter what you face, be the coffee bean.

Be Self-Aware and Respond to Your Feelings

I had been working in one company for about four-and-a-half years when I started to feel a bit disenchanted and could not quite understand why. I had held several roles through this time and moved up the corporate ladder along the way, yet something just wasn't right, and it left me with a very uncomfortable feeling. I was doing a senior sales role for an electronic banking business and everything on the outside seemed to be going well. The job required me to be a confrontational negotiator at times, but my preference and authentic style is to build consensus, so everyone feels like they are getting something of value. I can negotiate aggressively at times if I have to, which is why I was good at my job. However, while some people love the tussle of a hard bargaining session, I grew tired of the contentiousness and aggressiveness involved. It just wasn't me. I felt pressured by the firm to strike a deal that made the company benefit more than the clients, but my preference was to have both parties feel like they benefitted equally as my experience taught me that this was always better in the long run.

When I reflected on the situation, I came to realize that I was not in the right role at all. Although I had the skills and abilities to do the job, and even excel in some cases, my motivation to do the job was waning as each consecutive month went by. I tried to take stock of the situation by making a pros-and-cons list but even that wasn't much help as the list seemed quite balanced at the time. Then I took some time to do a bit of deeper soul searching and after completing that activity over a period of a few months, I determined that the job I was doing was not aligned to who I was as a person deep within my core. The values I needed to succeed in the job were often conflicting with my own personal values which, in a way, define who I am and what I stand for. The whole situation made me think about my self-identity ... not the superficial stuff on the surface, but the important inner stuff that acts as a moral compass through our lives. I determined that when an appropriate opportunity presented itself, I would transition to a new role, and I started to keep my eyes open for something that better aligned with my core values, key drivers, and personal motivators. Since then, I have always tried to make time every so often to constructively question my identity, thus continuously increasing my own self-awareness to help make me a better leader.

Do You Know Who You *Really* Are?

Do you know who you truly are? You go through life receiving messages, both conscious and unconscious, about the kind of person you ought to be. In college or university, your independence and sense of identity may have started to assert itself more as choices and behaviors became more individualized. However, there was still a strong element of acting and behaving in a certain way to fit in with the social group you chose to be a part of or naturally integrated into. And this may have extended into your early career years when fitting in and assimilating effectively into your work environment and peer community based on a new set of workplace norms and customs may have been important to help make the adjustment to "adult life" and navigate the sometimes sensitive transition from dependence on others to self-reliance and independence.

I recall my early university days when I felt significant pressure to behave in a certain way that was expected by other students in my cultural community. I was often invited to participate in certain cultural and religious gatherings with other members of the community. Although I was grateful for the invitation, this was at odds with who I was. Although I seemed to be part of a particular cultural community by virtue of my place of birth and some visible diversity characteristics, the reality was that I did not fit in with that community and felt an outsider because their customs and traditions were not my own. In the South Asian (Indian) community to which I belong by virtue of my birthplace and heritage, there are many faith communities including Hindu, Muslim, Sikh, and Christian. In this situation, it was about getting together with others for a puja, a group gathering of prayer, which is commonplace in the Hindu community. But all through my childhood years and while growing up, my family had never engaged in this tradition because, well, we were not actually part of this faith community—I am Christian and have been since my birth—but it's very hard to differentiate faith communities when people share the same skin color and social expectations based on shared visible diversity characteristics can complicate things at times. I tried for quite some time to be kind and respectfully decline. A couple of times I even agreed to participate for fear of offending my friends and because I wanted to fit in and be part of a supportive community. But in the end, I realized that to participate in this tradition felt inauthentic and I would not be living my life being true to myself. I also experienced this dynamic through some of my social communities and circles of friends. Although on the outside we had many similar qualities and aspirations, the fact is that I am quite a different type of person compared to many of my friends. By accepting who I genuinely am, I have been able to, over time, see beyond the peer pressure to do certain things, to dress a certain way, to socialize with certain types of people, and to aspire to partner with specific types of partner profiles (oh the horrible pressures of trying to find a life mate). I have more clarity and understanding of who I am at my core, which gives me a type of inner calm and self-confidence to be my authentic self.

After years of unconscious conditioning through the messages received from external sources, you have probably come to believe that you have a fairly good idea of who you are and what you're all about. But is this really you? Or is this the person you have been conditioned to think you should be? Do you know—*truly know*—and understand who you are … at your core? These are fundamental questions every person should ask themselves regularly throughout their lives. Asking yourself the question "Who am I?" is the starting point of living a leadership lifestyle. Sometimes, it's not a question that can be easily answered and requires some deep and considered reflection to be able to answer. Being honest with yourself about who you truly are will liberate you and give you a renewed sense of identity, a renewed sense of being, and a renewed sense of purpose that will lead you along the road to personal success and achievement.

Exploring a New Role

Returning to the story at the start of this Insight, after I transitioned out of the role that I felt didn't align with my values, I managed to find a temporary role that both energized and inspired me. I assumed a contract position working for a charitable organization that had a mission to help develop young people. This was something very important to me personally because of the own development opportunities I had through my younger years, and it aligned nicely with my core values. Although it was a temporary role, it gave me the chance to experiment with something that helped reaffirm my genuine identity and this helped build my self-awareness by teaching me that I needed to factor in my core values in future career endeavors in order to feel fulfilled. The role even gave me the opportunity to put my previous corporate skills to great use, so I felt like I was making a significant contribution from very early on, which only boosted my confidence and validated my belief that I had made the right choice to leave my previous role. All things considered that specific transition ended up being one of the most memorable experiences of my life since it enabled me to meet Pope John Paul II, a great spiritual leader of one of the world's religious faiths—all because I had taken the time to raise my own self-awareness and be true to my genuine self.

This experience, however, came with a variety of mixed emotions. I felt sad that I had left some of my previous colleagues, which made it more difficult to stay in touch with work friends. I felt proud of myself for having the courage to leave a very financially comfortable situation and head into a very uncertain temporary situation. I felt satisfaction because I had found a place and a role that strongly aligned with my values, and this provided me with a sense of purpose—I felt like I was making a difference. I also felt fear as I had walked away from financial stability to follow my heart in this instance. These emotions created both anxiety and joy, and years later I came to realize how the power of that transitional experience had truly benefited me; it helped me grow in ways I would never have been able to, had I stayed where I was and tried to live my life in a way that was not genuine to who I truly am.

15 Self-Awareness Questions for You to Answer

Knowing yourself is the first step in the journey to living a leadership lifestyle, because you have to know where you're starting from in order to figure out where you're going and how to get there. Here are 15 questions that will help you discover who you really are:

1. What are your core values?
2. What are your key motivations?
3. What are your strengths and weaknesses?
4. What are you passionate about?
5. What is truly important to you?
6. What are your hopes and dreams?
7. What are your limitations?
8. What are your fears? Where do these fears come from?
9. Who or what are the key influences in your life?
10. Who are the people that matter most in your life?
11. Why do these people matter so much to you?
12. How do you see yourself?
13. How do other people see you?
14. How do the answers to all these questions compare or contrast with how you live your life daily?
15. Are you living authentically and being true to yourself?

As you can see, truly knowing who you are requires serious self-reflection and only you can answer those questions truthfully. These questions have certainly helped me make the right decisions or right choices so I could stay true to myself. For example:

- When I ask myself what my key *motivations* are, I realize that it's rarely about financial gain but mostly about helping others to improve their personal circumstances in life through education and personal development experiences, because I had those kinds of opportunities throughout my life.

- When I ask myself what my *fears* are and where they come from, I realize that they are often financial fears as a direct result of some of the financial difficulties my family was faced with when I was a child after my own father died at a very young age. Knowing this is the source of my fears helps me to contain my anxiety. I think about the many financial challenges I've had through my life and remind myself that I got through them just fine. Each time, I stabilize the situation and with flexibility, adjust my lifestyle as needed to get through the hard times. This provides a sense of calm as well as hope for the future.

- When I reflect on the *key influences* in my life, I realize that they have been experiences and people who have touched my heart rather than change my thinking.

- And finally, when I ask myself why connecting meaningfully with other *people* means so much to me, I understand that it's not financial success that makes me truly happy inside; it's the key relationships I've developed and experiences I've shared with family and those in my closest circles. Those relationships and experiences inspire me to think about others and how my attitudes and actions may affect them.

Having these insights about myself have helped increase my self-awareness about who I genuinely am, which has helped guide my decisions and choices in ways that have brought more happiness and fulfillment into my life.

How We See Ourselves

Knowing and accepting who you really are is the first step to living a leadership lifestyle and becoming a truly great leader. But knowing yourself is easier said than done. We all like to think that we know who we are and that we know ourselves best, but part of the difficulty we face on a daily basis is that we, as human beings, see things the way we want to see them. Let's face it, nobody wants to see themselves as less than perfect. We all want to see ourselves as accomplished in some way with promising futures. We all want to see ourselves as successful, happy, and loved. We all want to see ourselves as belonging to various communities. It's just human nature. But sometimes, how we see ourselves is not how others see us. You can gain great insight into who you really are by learning how other people perceive you. I'm not suggesting that how others see you is necessarily an accurate indication of who you are, but it can be helpful from time to time. Knowing how others see you may give you valuable insights into how you portray yourself externally to the world around you. There is no right answer of course … *you are who you are*, and *you are how you are*. But getting a variety of perspectives may help you see yourself in ways you did not think of before and these insights could open the door to numerous possibilities that could raise your self-awareness and help guide you to great places.

Creating your **genuine identity profile** can be a helpful exercise to gain and improve your self-awareness. There are five key components to developing your genuine identity profile but the requirement for each of those components remains constant—you have to be totally honest with yourself right from the start. The five components are as follows:

1. **Self-Identity Statement.** Your self-identity statement can be a sentence or two summarizing your identity as you currently perceive it. Once completed, share the statement with people in your close circle whom you trust and respect, and tell them what you're trying to do. See how they react to your statement and solicit their input to help you refine your statement of self-identity. Ask them to be honest with you and explain that this is a learning and development exercise, and their honest input will help you to grow as a person. Do this

with several people and record the feedback you get. Then review all the comments and update your statement of identity if you think appropriate with your newly gained insights. Now comes the hard part … ask yourself if you agree with all the feedback you received? It may be easier to dismiss things you did not see or realize for yourself but before being so quick to dismiss anything, reflect on the things you did not see or realize before and question in your mind why you did not see these elements while other people did. This personal reflection is a powerful and liberating activity as it helps you gain insights and a context for who you really are.

2. **Core Values List.** The second thing you can do to help you gain self-awareness is making *a list of your core values.* Lists such as this can be long and rambling, so the task at hand here is for you to determine your top 8 to 10 core values that you consider the fabric of your being. After listing your top core values, make a note next to each core value on how you define it, what it means to you personally, and why it's important to you. Don't be fooled, this task may sound easy to complete but many people find it difficult to limit their list to just the top 8 to 10. And now comes the hard part, once you've completed your list of your top core values, ranking them in order of importance with number 1 being your most important core value. Make a note of how long it takes you to complete this portion of the task and once completed, reflect on the time it took you to finish. Did you get through it very quickly? Did it take you longer than you imagined it would? Were you conflicted while completing this exercise? Do any of your core values surprise you? Does the ranking surprise you in any way? Most importantly, when you go through the list of your core values, you know you've completed the task correctly if for each of the values, you can see a plethora of examples from your daily life. Once you are satisfied with your list, add the list of your core values below your statement of identity and see how your genuine identity profile starts to take shape.

3. **Most Important Things in Life List.** The third thing you can do to gain a better awareness of who you really are is to identify *the things in life that are most important to you.* Similar to the core

values list, you have to be vigilant; select only the top 3 to 5 things of importance, for if the list is too long, the importance of each gets diluted. Once you have listed the top 3 to 5 things of true importance to you, explain why each of these are important and then rank the list with number 1 being the most important. Once completed, add the list to the bottom of your genuine identity profile.

4. **Living Life Statement.** The fourth thing needed to help you complete your genuine identity profile is a statement *articulating how you want to live your life.* For example, do you want to get ahead no matter what the cost to other people or do you want to move forward in life in an ethical and meritocratic way? Okay, this was a very leading question, but you get the idea. Will you sacrifice whatever you need to in order to succeed or will you make considered decisions in alignment with your core values to help your move in the direction you want to go in life. It might be a good idea to make a list within this section of some of the things you may be willing to sacrifice in order to achieve your goals. For example, maybe you would like to travel but you will put aside travel to focus on your work. Or maybe your family and friends are important, but if you have to move far away to receive the best education or as a great career move, you will. Remember that there is no right answer, just your answer and it's important to be genuinely honest with yourself about how you want to live your life. When I accepted my very first full-time job, I had to leave my life behind and move to Japan. Although it was very exciting, it was also very challenging and difficult as I had to leave my family, friends, and my entire way of life behind. It was inevitable that I would struggle at times, but I was not prepared for how often this would happen. But in the end, I kept my focus on my desire to embrace new experiences to help me grow and develop as a leader and this helped to get me through the rough patches.

5. **Personal Impact Statement.** Finally, the fifth element needed to complete your genuine identity profile is a *statement of impact* that describes the impact you want to have in society. This may not be easy for many people, especially if you've never stopped to think

about this before. One way to articulate this statement is to ask yourself, "how do I want to be remembered?" and then use your answer as your statement of impact.

Developing your genuine identity profile will help you gain a better awareness of self. Through developing and reflecting upon the five components of your genuine identity profile—your statement of self, your core values, the things truly important to you, how you want to live your life, and your desired impact in society—you will gain self-awareness insights that will serve as an internal compass for you and provide direction and guidance to help you develop personally and move toward achieving your goals.

Here is an example of how you can work through the exercise.

Statement of Self-Identity

I am a loving and committed father and husband who wants the best for his children and family, with a love for outdoor adventures. Professionally, I am a marketing manager who specializes in new product development, who enjoys working in a collegiate and collaborate way.

Core Values List (in Order of Importance)

i. Integrity—being truthful, trustworthy, and open. This is important to me both personally and professionally.

ii. Honesty—related to the abovementioned integrity for the same reasons.

iii. Happiness—being in a state where you are not sad or upset and are pleased with your lot. Ultimately this is very important to me, but I don't think you can have happiness with others unless you have integrity and are honest.

iv. Loyalty—sticking by people, even when times are tough. It means a lot to me for me not to be flaky and for others to be loyal to me.

v. Responsibility—making sure you get the job done—again it's important to me because I value colleagues and family doing what they say they will and seeing it through.

   vi. Caring—caring about the well-being of myself and others and quality of what you are doing. It's important to me that people take care over what they do.

  vii. Fairness—being equal or fair-minded. It's important to me that I am treated fairly because I feel that it's equally important to treat others fairly.

 viii. Stability—having certainty and surety. I like to be sure and certain in what I do and where I am headed.

Most Important Things in Life List

    i. My health—without your health you cannot help others and achieve your aims.

   ii. My partner and children—it's important to me to do the best for my children and family. I want my children to get a good education and to set them up well to have the skills they need for life.

  iii. My parents (and wider family)—family is important to me.

  iv. Being financially secure and having a comfortable life and retirement. While material possessions are not as important as the abovementioned, I would like to have a certain standard of living.

   v. Being fit—it's important to be physically and mentally fit.

Living Life Statement

I want to have a balanced life, working hard when needed, but not too hard and not to the detriment of my health and family relationships. I want my life to be balanced in all ways, including health, diet, fitness, time at work, holidays, and so on. I want to have integrity and to be happy.

Personal Impact Statement

I don't need to have any big impact on society or to be famous in any way. I would like to be remembered for being a good family man, loyal to my wife and children, and doing the best for my family.

Leadership Lifestyle Exercise:
Your Genuine Identity Profile

Take a moment now to reflect on your own identity. Then, using the previous structure, create your own genuine identity profile and keep it close by at all times so you can refer to it as needed to remind yourself of who you really are.

Build and Protect Your Personal Brand

Although we mostly associate brands with tangible products or services, a person can also have a brand. Your brand represents everything about you to the people around you. It is how you are perceived by others. The more familiar manifestation of your personal brand is known as your "reputation." Your own self-perception, including your perception of your reputation, is important. What also counts, however, is what others think, because their perception of you demonstrates how you bring your brand to life.

The Ambassador's Insight

I first learned about the concept of a personal brand in a *Fast Company* magazine article during the summer of 1997. I had recently completed my MBA but had not come across the concept of a personal brand for an individual, having only had exposure to brands in relation to products being sold and consumer purchase habits. I was intrigued, and the notion of a personal brand has stayed with me ever since. Around that time, I was sharing a large house with some university friends in order to save money to help pay off my student debt. One of my new housemates was the son of the Italian Ambassador to Canada at the time. Giovanni and I became good friends over the following months and his parents got to know me and appreciate the friendship we had developed. Later that year, I was invited to celebrate the Easter holiday with his family at the Ambassador's residence in Ottawa. It was an intimate gathering of only family, and I felt humbled and honored to have been invited for the family gathering.

I remember sitting at the dining table and the Ambassador telling me how happy he was that I was able to join his family that weekend. Because of their globally mobile lifestyle, the Ambassador explained to me—an occupational hazard no doubt for any diplomat and their family—his children usually did not get a chance to establish meaningful friendships with people. He felt very happy that his son and I had become friends because he thought I had a positive influence on him.

And after a few more hours of conversation through the afternoon and feasting on a wonderful family meal, he also shared with me that he thought I had a talent for being able to see things through the eyes of others and that this would serve me well in my life. That was the moment I started to become aware of my own personal brand. I have since come to include this ability to see situations from multiple perspectives whenever I think about my own personal brand. When I reflect on my brand, I notice a strong alignment to the values identified when completing my own genuine identity profile as discussed in the previous chapter. The self-awareness gained by completing that exercise has informed my personal brand identity and this synergy provides a solid foundation to live a leadership lifestyle. I continuously keep my own personal brand top of mind, which helps me to preserve and promote my genuine identity through everything I do.

When was the last time you stopped to think about your own personal brand? Thinking about and building a personal brand is not typically high on most people's to-do lists. Businesses hire teams of people to maintain their brand because it takes a lot of work. However, to build and maintain your personal brand, you don't need to rely on anyone else except yourself. You have full control and accountability for your brand and how it is maintained and protected. This is incredibly empowering, but it can also be incredibly daunting; if anything goes wrong, you'll only have yourself to blame.

Branding Mistakes

No one is perfect and you are bound to make a few mistakes along the way while building your own personal brand. After all, even huge brands can make a mistake. One example of a brand miscue is the Super League debacle in European football in 2021. Teams such as Liverpool and Real Madrid proposed an elite football league made only of the best teams in Europe. Fans erupted in protest, hammering the greed behind the proposal. The teams viewed themselves as Elite European Teams, rather than members of their nation's football leagues. Massive fan protests quickly set the teams back on course.

A little closer to home in my own life, in the early days of my personal brand awareness, I made many mistakes trying to apply my personal brand to the circumstances I was in. I knew that I was willing to work hard to earn a good reputation that would open doors for me and get me recognized as dedicated and reliable. Somewhere along the way, however, I started to think that recognition and support would happen automatically if people liked me, and I started to behave in ways that would endear me to others, rather than earn their respect. Soon I found that I was trying so hard to please others that I was exhausting myself in the process, which meant I wasn't getting the job done. As human beings, I think we all may struggle at times with working hard to please others and losing sight of what's important. I became aware of what was happening by taking time to reflect on my personal brand and assess how I was living that brand. Through this experience, I learned that building time into your regular routines to focus on your personal brand is a helpful way to help you maintain it and stay true to your goals.

Protecting Your Personal Brand

Another important consideration is how to *protect* your personal brand. While we may not think this is necessary when we establish our brand, it's easy to get derailed and stray off course through the many distractions and sometimes competing priorities that life sends our way. Protecting your personal brand means not only understanding what you must do and how you must live your life but also means having an awareness of what *not* to do and what you should stay away from.

Social media, for example, can harm your brand. We all get the impulse every now and then to throw our two cents worth into an online dialogue about things we may be passionate about. In some ways this is a good thing, as it shows we have an opinion and want to share that opinion. But be mindful that this can also work against you if you chime in on things that you may not be an expert on nor qualified enough to speak definitively about. And it can be especially harmful to your long-term success if your comments are hurtful to others, or incorrect factually. There are myriad examples of employees who have been fired after posting insensitive or insulting comments on the Facebook page or on Twitter.

Commenting on what your network contacts may have written about can be a good way to show support for others, but if you want to protect your own personal brand, stop for a moment, and reflect on what you're about to post. Consider your comments carefully and ask yourself if your comments will help strengthen your own personal brand or hinder the brand you're trying to maintain. Then decide how you want to proceed, again taking ownership of the consequences that may result. It's often the little things that help you the most to maintain and protect your brand, so be mindful as much as possible on your personal brand and how your actions and behaviors may impact it.

Thoughtful Personal Branding

Building your brand is not only about what you do, but how you do it. For example, you may complete your tasks on time and be well prepared for meetings. However, if you accomplish this by withholding information from others and hoarding resources, which causes others to fall behind schedule, you're actually destroying your brand, not building it. Remember that personal brand building is about what you do *and* how you do it.

When I was trying to establish my own brand in my early career days, I was too focused internally (some may call this my tunnel vision); I could easily have been described as having a one-track mind. I failed to consider that I was not operating in a vacuum and that my own brand-building actions had an impact on others, sometimes good and sometimes bad. I had a rude awakening one day when one of my friends had the courage to let me know that he thought I was becoming conceited because of the way I would go on about some of the good things happening in my life at the time. I was so shocked … I hadn't realized this was how I was coming across. I thought I was simply sharing stories from my work life with others, but I did not stop to think about how others would be receiving the information I was putting out. I immediately thought back to the words of the Ambassador who complimented me on my ability to see situations through many perspectives—clearly, I had let that slip. I felt awful and disappointed in myself. I realized that in some circumstances, my efforts to build my personal brand were having a negative impact on others I cared about. Since then, I have tried to think about others as much as possible and then decide how to move forward effectively. My brand is about helping people, not hurting them, and at times this means I must make difficult choices and adapt my actions to achieve my personal brand goals.

In building your brand, language—both verbal and body language— can be a huge asset. To constantly reinforce your brand message to yourself and others, be aware of how you communicate with others, consciously trying to communicate in a manner that aligns with the personal brand you want to achieve. In no time at all, your personal brand will start to take shape and your actions for brand maintenance and protection will become second nature.

For example, how do you communicate your accomplishments? It's important to feel proud of what you've achieved as this reinforces your self-confidence. However, if others were also involved in the success, do you talk about what "you" did or what "we" did? That is, do you take full credit for the success, or do you ensure that people know that the success came about through the efforts of others as well? If you are always talking about *your* success and not *our* success, you are destroying any chance of having "team player" as part of your brand.

Your words as well as your actions will either reinforce or weaken the brand you want to create for yourself. Remember: be a brand maker, not a brand breaker!

So how do you set about building your brand? As a consultant, one activity I have found that helps many people is a short brand-building exercise that requires you to first define the brand you want to create for yourself, and then break down the various things you need to do on a consistent basis to establish, build, and protect your brand.

Leadership Lifestyle Exercise:
Build Your Personal Brand

The first step in building your personal brand is to select a list of five words that will characterize your brand. Examples include trustworthy, professional, reliable, collaborative, and sincere. If you're having difficulty coming up with the list of characteristics, just try to complete the following sentence:

"(Your name) is known for being _____."

If you can come up with a list of five words, then you're well on your way to defining your personal brand. Over the course of this exercise, this list may change several times. Not a problem. The more words you can come up with, the better, as it will demonstrate just how difficult it can be to establish a personal brand. You just have to make sure to pick the five words that best exemplify the brand you want to create for yourself.

Once the list of five words has been finalized, the next step is to come up with four to five actions for each characteristic that consistently demonstrates to others you are living that characteristic. If you maintain these actions, you will, over time, come to be known for that characteristic.

For example, if you select "professional" as one of your personal brand characteristics, you may come up with the following actions to externally portray yourself as "professional":

1. You are punctual and well prepared when you attend meetings.
2. You work hard, complete all tasks on time, and work well in a team.

---

3. You respect others and never gossip in the workplace.

4. You follow up with others in a timely manner.

5. You consistently provide more than what is expected.

Complete five action points for each brand characteristic. Get started as soon as possible: Building a personal brand takes time.

INSIGHT 4

Trust Your Instincts. Listen to Your Inner Voice

When it was time to buy my first home, I was filled with fear and anxiety. For most people, buying a home is the largest investment and outlay of financial resources they will ever make. I tried to prepare myself by researching all I could about how to make a good home-buying decision and what criteria to look for. I watched so many property-related programs and talked to many experienced professionals in property circles whom I knew to learn all I could. But when the time came, understandably, I still had the fear and, in a way, I was in a position of vulnerability. One of the things I learned was that when you're buying your first home, you should try and stretch yourself as much as possible and make as many sacrifices you can in the early days of your home ownership as it will pay off down the road later in life. I was so hesitant as I don't like to take on too much financial risk, but my inner voice was telling me that when it comes to buying the home I had identified—having done all my homework and due diligence and selecting a property that made sense to purchase both on paper, and emotionally for my happiness—that this was a risk worth taking so I went ahead with the purchase. Thank goodness I did. I ended up buying a new build property straight off the plans the developer had provided. It's always a risk doing this because you can't really see what you're buying, and things could change through the build. But it was the combination of the property itself and the location that I was taking a risk on and within about six weeks of signing the purchase contract, the property developer came back to me and offered to buy the property back from me for £25,000 more that I would be paying for it. Now by any standards earning £25K in a six-week period is good, but the circumstances had helped me realize that I had made a good decision and I should hang on to it rather than sell and take a quick win. Over time this has worked out for me as my home equity continued to grow and grow, as the housing market improved year after year. My inner voice steered me in the right direction, despite some messages tempting me to do something else.

Your Inner Voice Is Instinctive

Whether you call it your instinct, your intuition, your sixth sense, or your gut feeling, listening to your inner voice is an important part of living a leadership lifestyle. Your inner voice is instinctive and often speaks to you when you are least expecting it. It has come to be akin to an internal compass of sorts. Sometimes your inner voice is providing guidance; sometimes your inner voice is warning you about something; sometimes your inner voice gives you a rationale for doing something you weren't quite so certain about by making you feel comfortable about an action you want to take; and sometimes your inner voice helps to bring clarity and context to confusing situations. Over time, many people come to trust their inner voice as their personal experience has proven it right or wrong. Learning how to interpret and listen to your inner voice can be one of the most powerful assets in your personal toolkit for living a leadership lifestyle and achieving your goals.

Ignoring the Inner Voice

Most people I meet tend to pay more attention to the messages they receive from the external world rather than listen to their own inner voice. This is especially problematic when these external messages are negative or in contradiction to one's inner voice and this sometimes has the effect of increasing self-doubt. Perhaps this is our survival instinct kicking in or perhaps we as humans tend to act out of fear when faced with adversity, difficulty, or challenge of any sort. When this occurs, we can, at times, self-sabotage our own success and happiness by not treating our own inner voice as an important data point that should be carefully factored into our decisions and actions.

One example of this in many people's lives is choosing a field of study for higher education. For example, your inner voice may tell you to study art or music in school because you are artistically talented—and you know that choosing this course of study will further develop your talent and make you happy. But pressure from others may lead you to choose economics, law, or science because of the financial realities of today's world. And even though you may get good results in your academic programmed, you are not fulfilled and don't look forward to working in the field you have studied.

A similar example is choosing a particular career path. You may be fortunate enough to have two job offers—one that you know will bring you happiness while the other may bring you greater wealth. If you were in this situation, which path would you choose? Most people tend to choose the one that leads to greater wealth. For some people, this may be the right decision as they find that they enjoy the trappings of financial success. Others may choose the path to greater wealth only to later find out that they are unhappy and feeling unfulfilled. They realize that their genuine identity and personal brand have less to do with financial wealth than they thought. Yet, they did not listen to their inner voice, choosing instead to heed the messages received from the external world, even though they knew deep down that their choice may not be the right decision for them.

But why don't we listen to our inner voice, our instincts, and gut feelings, when these messages and cues guide us? Sometimes we come to a crossroads in our life where we know instinctively that taking one course of action will be better for us, yet we may choose not to listen to our inner voice and take a different course of action. Your inner voice tells you to choose the path of happiness because you are more likely to be successful at a career you are highly motivated to be in, but you end up choosing the career that brings you more financial wealth because your fear or pressure from others influences you to choose the safer and easier path in life. In essence, we sometimes choose to ignore our inner voice altogether because our inner voice may lead us toward a more difficult path, even though it feels intrinsically right for us. This course of action may bring you comfort temporarily but will not necessarily bring you happiness and success.

When I was in my early 20s, I was lucky enough to get a tax refund of slightly over $1,500 one year. It was such a welcome surprise and I wanted to do something constructive with it, so I decided to invest in the stock market. At the time, I had not known too much about how to invest effectively (one can argue that I'm still in that same position now) but I decided that I was going to take the risk and I invested in some popular technology stocks that were the talk of the market at the time. At first, I was so happy because the stocks increased in value month by month and that small sum of money I started with had multiplied significantly. My inner voice was telling me that I should cash out while I was ahead by selling the shares and taking my profit. But perhaps I became a bit greedy as I did not do what my inner voice was telling me to do, thinking that my shares would continue to increase in value, and I could make even more profit. I guess you can figure out how this story ends ... a few weeks later there was a shock in the financial markets and the value of my shares tanked so badly that by the time I was able to sell them, I had ended up with just a small fraction of what I had started out with. My inner voice was telling me to do something, but I did not listen ... and I paid the price!

Inner Voice Versus External Hard Data

Deciding whether to believe our inner voice is a choice. Unfortunately, many people don't even believe in the validity of their inner voice. They may acknowledge it, but then tend to discount it or reason it away. There's an internal dilemma, an invisible struggle between our inner voice, which can be a very positive influence, and the many external messages hurled our way from the external world that pressure us to go in a different direction.

These external messages have a hold on us because society tends to focus on hard evidence much more than it does intangible evidence. Less value is placed on soft data such as feelings and emotions when compared to hard data that is quantifiable and often used as definitive evidence, and this is often considered more valid than data that cannot be measured easily nor accurately. Inundated for years with messages that reinforce this acceptance of hard data over soft data leads us to accept this bias over time. For example, we measure grades in school, we seek to acquire more and more followers in our social media accounts, we quest for more "likes" as a form of acknowledgment from others. We live in a culture of quantifiables, relevant metrics, performance dashboards, and a culture of ticking boxes and measuring things that tend to have a yes/no answer. As for my forays into the stock market now, I've learned to truly listen to my inner voice as much as the technical fundamentals of stock prices. Of course, I still make some mistakes here and there—after all, nobody has a crystal ball. But I've learned to listen to my inner voice and if it tells me, it's time to cash out, I usually do. I've learned the value of taking a "good enough" profit rather than taking one-too-many risks to try and get the best return. This strategy has paid off me over time. Being able to take a good enough profit is much better than taking no profit at all or even worse, making a loss.

But as we all know, life is not always that simple and the choices we have to make are not always black or white. There's a reason the expression "shades of grey" exists in our everyday vernacular. Your inner voice may be difficult to quantify, but it provides just as much evidence and information as something that can be easily measured. In fact, your inner voice sometimes provides more information than hard evidence can provide because the data you receive from your inner voice helps you to translate the evidence into information that helps you to decide what to do next, given your own specific circumstances and in relation to your genuine identity. When you listen to your inner voice, your decisions are aligned with your core values, key motivators, and personal drivers, and also take into account your own personal brand. The only problem is, we are so conditioned to only listen to negative messages from the outside world rather than what our inner voice tells us that we often reject the constructive messages we receive from our inner voice, and this can sometimes hold us back from achieving our goals.

The Subtle Clue You May Be Missing

Transforming your instinct for survival into your instinct for success also means consciously paying more attention to the constructive messages and cues your inner voice gives you. So many times in our lives we get these messages but fail to take notice of them for whatever reason. Yet if we were more consciously aware of these messages and listened to them more often, we would surely begin to understand ourselves a lot better and build the confidence we need to pursue our goals with greater clarity of purpose.

People often do things that make them feel good, but they fail to recognize the good feeling as a cue for success. If you're not listening to your inner voice, you're failing to hear the important messages being provided to you. For example, you may be developing your talents further through art or music, which you enjoy and excel at, yet you can't see this as a sign that perhaps this activity should play a greater role in your life. You may be giving of your time to work with charitable organizations and get enriched by the experience of working to help others in need, yet you don't recognize this as a sign that maybe you're in the wrong career and need to make a change that will both help others and make you feel more fulfilled in your life.

It may be helping young people learn new things by volunteering in your child's school, or it may be a longing to live an entirely different kind of lifestyle, so radically opposite to the one you're currently living, that the thought of it seems ridiculous, impossible, and fills you with self-doubt about your ability to achieve such a transformation and instils a sense of fear that paralyzes from taking any action to move in that direction. If your inner voice is telling you something, it is probably for a good reason!

Inner Voice and Career Success

When I first moved to the United Kingdom in 2003 without having any job lined up, you can imagine the mixture of emotions that came along with me. I was so happy to have this great new life experience, but at the same time there was significant financial stress and worry as I had to stabilize my circumstances as quickly as possible as I was living in one of the most expensive cities in the world. I interviewed with some firms and after a few short months, I received a job offer that would have significantly made my new life easier. But somehow deep within me it just did not feel right. The company focused its work that was not an area of interest or expertise for me, and I had a dilemma trying to decide whether to accept the role or not. My inner voice was telling me that although life would be easier, this role would not be right for me and would not bring happiness into my life. If anything, I would end up feeling more regret and start to hate myself for making a wrong decision, simply to take an easier path. I ended up declining the offer and life for the next few months was very difficult for me. The financial stress and the sacrifices I had to make put me to the test. But before long, another opportunity surfaced, and it was much more interesting and more suitable for me, so I accepted and never looked back. My inner voice helped me by acting as a guide for what is right … maybe not right for everyone, but definitely right for me.

If you are going to succeed you must develop the ability to listen to your inner voice and be comfortable with what it is saying so you can learn how to transform your instinct for survival into your instinct for success. Acknowledge the message, listen to the message, reflect on it carefully, then try and come up with viewpoints that counter the contradicting messages you receive from the external world so you're able to see the situation differently. Once you're comfortable that you've looked at the situation from different perspectives, then charge ahead with a course of action that you feel more confident with. There will always be an important place and purpose for the messages you receive from the outside, but you must compliment this with the messages your inner voice may give you.

Leadership Lifestyle Exercise: Identifying Your Inner Voice

Your inner voice can be an important asset for you to successfully lead a leadership lifestyle but for some people being able to identify your inner voice can be difficult. It's not actually a "voice" like you hear when someone is speaking to you … although it can be sometimes.

(Continues)

(*Continued*)

Your inner voice has many forms, so this short exercise is aimed at helping you identify the moments when your inner voice is trying to tell you something. Try this short reflective exercise to determine how your inner voice speaks to you and add to the list if your inner voice manifests in other ways not mentioned here.

1. Do you sometime hear a quiet voice or imagine someone (maybe even yourself) trying to give yourself advice on what to do (or what not to do) in a particular situation?
2. Do you get a funny feeling in your stomach sometimes or feel nervous about something?
3. Do you have trouble sleeping sometimes or have bizarre dreams during times when you're facing challenges or difficulties, or when you have an important decision to make?
4. Do you find yourself on edge or particularly moody or emotionally sensitive at times when you feel less in control?
5. Do you find yourself seeking out more and more information, never feeling like you have enough to base a decision on?

These are just some of the ways your inner voice may be trying to speak to you, but it is by no means an exhaustive list. If and when these things happen, take a moment to calm down if you need to and reflect on why you might be experiencing these symptoms.

What's going on in your life during these times? Do you feel comfortable at how things are going or distressed because of a misalignment of how things are progressing compared to your core values as identified in your Genuine Identity Profile.

Make note of these things so you can try and identify the moments your inner voice may be speaking to you a lot sooner the next time it happens. This will help you factor in the information you are receiving and integrate it into your thoughts and decision-making behaviors so you can move forward feeling confident you've examined the situation from a hard data perspective as well as the soft data received. It makes for a more well-rounded decision.

And remember that if you think your inner voice manifests itself to you in other ways, make note of that too to increase your self-awareness!

INSIGHT 5

Visualize. Plan. Act.

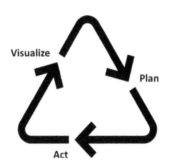

There can be no progress and no success if you don't take action. A leadership lifestyle is a lifestyle of action—which does not mean a lifestyle of impulse. Thoughtful action is a three-step process:

1. Visualize your action and its outcome.
2. Plan thoroughly.
3. Take action.

Visualize Your Outcome

No matter what goal you are trying to achieve as a leader, it all begins with a clear vision of what you want. This is called visualization and its power should not be underestimated. Many of us have heard stories of successful athletes who, in addition to training their bodies to improve physical conditioning, also train their minds on an ongoing basis to focus on a clear vision of their success. In essence, they can *see* themselves at the top of the ranks achieving their goal and this training helps to reinforce the self-confidence necessary to succeed at the task at hand. Although there may be different kinds of goals—for example, a goal to be CEO by the time you're 35 years old versus the goal to find a job in a new city—this technique of visualization is relevant and can be applied to almost all types of goals you can imagine. It's the concept and the act of visualization that's important here, not the goal itself.

There are many ways to visualize your goals. For some people, it's as simple as spending a few minutes each day thinking about what they want to achieve. Their visualization takes place in their minds. Others who may need to see things more tangibly will cut out images from magazines and newspapers that represent what they are trying to achieve and create a scrapbook or storyboard to help bring their vision to life. For example, a young professional may want to someday reach the highest levels of an international corporation. That young professional may periodically make a deliberate effort to imagine him- or herself in a C-suite boardroom, contributing to major strategic decisions for the global firm. Or the young professional may create a scrapbook of the headquarters of major firms—photos of a London skyscraper or a Silicon Valley campus or the sprawling headquarters in a mid-sized city—corporate headquarters for even the largest of corporations are varied.

Some people need to tell others about what they are trying to achieve and talk about it as much as possible, while others may need to draw pictures or create charts to help them bring to life the things they are trying to accomplish. Is there any one correct way to visualize your goals? Not really. It's different for everyone so you're free to find a way that works best for you. What's important, however, is the act of visualization because it helps you to gain clarity on what you're trying to achieve. Once you gain this clarity, you will be able to plan a course of action that takes you in the desired direction that moves you closer toward your goal.

Plan Thoroughly

One of my favorite motivational quotations is, "A goal without a plan is just a wish." If you are going to achieve your goals, it's helpful if you develop a plan outlining how you're going to do so. All it takes is a little focus, thoughtfulness, and of course, some investment in time to map out your plan so it becomes a good reference to revisit periodically when you need to make sure you're on track. It might sound like a bit of work, but it can also be quite a fun and imaginative exercise to complete—and a helpful and important one—as well as it will enable you to focus on your efforts, and in many cases preserve your resources. As a result, you will be spending your time and energy on things that really matter and you'll be able to achieve your stated goal quicker, instead of wasting your time and resources on things that will not get you to where you want to be.

If you don't make a plan, you're likely to be trying everything that remotely offers the possibility of taking you closer to success. This is not the best way to move forward with your plans as you will waste a lot of energy, both mental and physical. It's more effective if you try to prioritize your efforts and tasks so that you are focusing on high-impact activities that can present opportunities to get you to your goal faster and in many cases offer multiple benefits or create more opportunities to shorten the distance to your dreams.

In 2001, I left a job in banking and took up a freelance position on a one-year contract to get a new professional experience as well as to give myself some time to figure out what I was going to do next. I had an amazing experience during that year, but I knew it was just an interim step. I really wanted to move to the United Kingdom and work in England so that I would have some European professional experience to complement my previous work experience in Asia, as well as my work experience from North America. I thought this would help to make me a well-rounded global professional and increase my marketability in the professional world. But having that goal required some planning because there were many different elements that needed to be sorted out. Where would I live? What about work visas? What was the right time to go and what would I do when I got there? All these questions were coming up in my mind over and over so I thought the best approach was to make a plan that I could follow to help me achieve my goal. My plan began with the basics and essentials: gaining entry to England to work legally; saving enough money so that I had something to live on as I looked for a new job; and doing extensive networking and job hunting from Canada to increase my chances of quickly finding a job when I arrived.

To be able to work legally in England, I investigated various visa scenarios for someone with my background and nationality and soon found an interesting new program that the UK government was trialing that would be perfect for someone like me, so I applied and got the visa with very little difficulty. Then I thought about where I would live in the early days after I arrived until I found my own place. Having traveled to England before, I knew it was expensive to stay in hotels and I would not be able to do this for more than a day or two. One of my friends from university was studying for his PhD in London at the time, so I contacted him to see if I could crash on his sofa for a couple of weeks until I found my own place. He was more than happy to help. Things started to fall into place but there was still some planning left to do.

To ensure that I had sufficient funds when I first arrived, I immediately began to save money as part of my "make-it-or-break-it" fund. By the time I was ready to go, I had saved up enough to last me for about six months, so that became my time frame.

Finally, during my year of preparation, I networked like crazy with professional contacts who were already in the United Kingdom in hopes that they may offer me a job. I also made several visits to London to meet with potential employers for interviews and to demonstrate how serious I was about making the move.

Another important question in planning this move was deciding when I should go. I started my exploration through 2002 and it took many months to get all the information I needed. But I was all set to go by the fall of that year. However, it was important for me to be with family during the Christmas period, so I decided to wait until the end of year and only go in January the following year. It was also a symbolic time for me as I would be starting a new chapter in my life, both personally and professionally, around the beginning of a new year, so it all seemed just right.

And the result? Well, it all worked out of course and I owe it all to the planning I did in advance, without which, I don't think I would have managed to succeed and achieve my goal.

What's In a Plan?

Now that we've discussed the importance of having a plan, the next step is determining what should be included in your plan. I'm a firm believer in keeping things simple. The simpler the better. One of the best ways I've developed truly effective plans is by going back to basics and using those all-important five Ws and H questions: Who? What? When? Where? Why? And How? Your plan does not have to be complicated at all, but it should help you outline what you need to do to help you achieve your goal. If you can find answers to the questions Who? What? When? Where? Why? And How? you now have the fundamentals of a good plan to achieve your goals. The more specific you can be when answering each of the questions, then the better your plan will be as it provides more clarity and detail about the things, you'll need to do to accomplish your goal.

Revisiting my own goal to work in the United Kingdom, my simple plan was as follows:

Who—I will start out staying with my friend for a couple of weeks until I found my own place to stay.

What—I am going to find a job in the United Kingdom, however at this time I don't know what that will be. That is my mission, and the variable that will make this a great adventure.

When—I am ready in the fall but want to wait until after Christmastime as it is important for me to be with my family for the holidays: I will move to the United Kingdom early in the new year.

Where—I will move to London, England. This is where my friend is located so I will have some form of a support network, and this is where most of the professional opportunities will be.

Why—I want to gain European work experience to compliment my Asian and North American work experience to make me a more well-rounded global professional.

How—I need to save money to have a "make-it-or-break-it" fund for me to survive on while I get established and I need to network and explore as many opportunities as possible prior to my arrival.

The Plan as Motivation

A great way to leverage your plan is to use your plan not only as a kind of roadmap to get you to success but also as an important motivational tool to keep you engaged, focused, and energized. The way to do this is by rearranging the information in your plan by deciding what's most important given your own personal circumstances. For example, you might be wanting to start a local charity to help fund research for a rare medical condition. Your driving force for this is that your young child has that rare medical condition and there are not many resources available to you for information or support.

An alternative way to create your plan could be to start by answering the question Why? first and then carry on with the other interrogatives in order of importance to you. The genesis of my move to England started with the why: to increase my marketability as a professional by complimenting my Asian and North American work experience with European work experience. In this example, every time I referred to my plan I reminded myself of the purpose of my goal and this was a powerful motivator during times that I felt success was slow to come. Having a powerful, detailed, and well-articulated plan is an important element in achieving your goals by allowing you to stay focused on prioritized, high-impact activities that will help you get to success faster.

Putting Your Plan Into Action

So now you've got a plan. Fantastic! But having a plan alone will not bring you any closer to success … it will just help you have more clarity on what success actually means—that is, being clearer on what you're trying to achieve and why, how, and so on. There's one more thing you have to do if you want to achieve your goals. If you want to be successful, you must put your plan into action. I shared one of my favorite quotes with you earlier in this chapter—"A goal without a plan is just a wish." I'd like to share one more saying with you now—"A plan without action is just a regret."

Implementing your plan effectively requires some advance thought and consideration if you're to be most effective. The best way to put your plan into action is to develop your "action plan" as a subset of the "When?" section of your goal plan. You should ensure that the detail includes a timeline that you can easily pull out of your plan and treat it as a tool that you will refer to and closely follow for you to focus your efforts and track your progress. Your timeline should clearly indicate the activities that need to be completed, and these activities should be listed sequentially in priority order. Next to each activity, you should identify any key dependencies or constraints that need to be taken into account. Next to that, you should clearly identify who the best person is to help you to complete that task (assuming you are able to enlist the help of others). Next to that you should put a target date for completing the task. Be realistic here as the last thing you want to do is set yourself up for disappointment by setting yourself a time frame that will be impossible to achieve. It will demotivate you and could set you back.

Finally, at the far right section of your action plan, indicate how you will know when you have completed the activity so you can track your progress and move on to the next task. Use your action plan as a kind of check list to keep you on track and to maintain a forward momentum that takes you closer and closer to achieving your goal—and continuously provides new motivation every time you complete a task that brings you closer to your goal.

This process of visualizing, planning, and acting is one I put into practice every time I set a goal for myself. Throughout my life it has proven to be a simple and effective way to be successful at whatever I set my mind to. One example of this was my determination to get into a top business school after many years of professional life. Just about 20 years had passed since I graduated with my MBA, so the thought of going back to school after so long was very daunting. However, it was a goal I set for myself to continue my lifelong learning.

In order to achieve the goal, I first visualized myself sitting in a lecture room at the school I wanted to attend. I had seen pictures of some classrooms on the Internet, so it was easy to visualize the surroundings, but I struggled at first to see myself sitting in one of the chairs in the lecture hall. But after trying for a while, I was able to see myself there, sitting and learning in a classroom with other like-minded people who also wanted to learn in a formal learning setting. When I had a clear picture and clarity of what I wanted to achieve, I made a plan that included all the elements written about a bit earlier in this section.

Finally, it was time to put my plan into action. After carefully planning to understand what I needed to do to accomplish the goal, I started to implement my plan in the steps I had outlined and before I knew it, that joyful day came when I got the communication from the school that my application was successful, and I was admitted. It was a great day and making my plan and putting it into action surely helped me to achieve my goal.

Leadership Lifestyle Exercises

Following are some simple templates to help you get organized for your own planning and action. Use the examples here to develop your own plans to achieve your goals. And remember to start off with your own visualization exercise, perhaps in your mind, or make a storyboard or collage as described at the beginning of this insight chapter.

1. **Simple and Effective Planning**—Populate the empty boxes by answering the questions

   You can switch the order of the items in the left column to make the plan more meaningful to you.

A simple template to help you clarify and set your own goals

Goal	(Write your goal in this section)
Who	Who is this goal for? Who can you think of that can help you in some way to achieve your goal?
What	What are trying to achieve? Try and be as specific as possible.
When	When is the right time to attempt this goal? Is there a wrong time that you should avoid if at all possible?
Where	Where does this goal happen?
Why	Why are you attempting this goal? What will be gained by striving to achieve this goal?
How	How can you prepare in advance to realize this goal? How can you make this process as smooth and effective as possible, so your time and energy are being used effectively?

2. **Action Planning**—Fill in the boxes to determine how to put your plan into action.

Try and make this plan as detailed as you possibly can ... the more detail you can include the better and easier it becomes to implement your plan as all the steps are outlined.

A simple tool to help you make your action plan

Task	Dependencies	Key People	Start Date	Completion Date	Success Measure
Task 1					
Task 2					
Task 3					
Task 4					
etc. etc. etc.					

INSIGHT 6

Accept That Risk Is Part of a Leadership Lifestyle

To succeed, you must accept that you will have to take risks in life and get out of your comfort zone from time to time. You will have to make the difficult choices that are needed and take *calculated* risks. It's all fine and dandy to dream big—to have ambition, aspiration, hope, and optimism. It's all fine and dandy to visualize and plan. But when it is time to take that next step and take action to move forward confidently in the direction of your dreams, you may feel the fear and apprehension that many do when they are about to embark on something new.

The good news is that this is normal. The discomfort, the unease, the hesitation. These are all human responses whenever risk and uncertainty are involved. The not-so-good news is that unless you can take that courageous next step and move forward toward your goals, you're just going to remain stagnant. Don't let anxiety stop you from taking any action at all—and ultimately stop you from achieving your goals.

When you become aware that taking risk is an essential part of living a leadership lifestyle, you also become aware that there will be consequences resulting from the risks you take. There are a number of actions you can take to mitigate the risks you take, thus reducing your fear of risk and overcoming the temptation to avoid risk altogether:

1. Give yourself permission to be afraid.
2. Think of positive outcomes.
3. Focus on the small steps.
4. Conduct due diligence.

Give Yourself Permission to Be Afraid

It's important to give yourself permission to be afraid. By giving yourself this permission and allowing yourself to be the human being you are, you psychologically regain control of the situation. A leadership lifestyle is one that accepts risk and respects risk while not letting the fear of risk dictate your decisions and actions. Risk in itself is a neutral thing; it's our perception and attitude toward risk that makes it good or bad. Accept that risk exists in life and embrace it as an opportunity to learn, develop, grow, overcome your fear, and break through your preconceived boundaries.

Think of Positive Outcomes

The hardest step you will ever have to take is the first one. All too often, we are stifled from taking any action that involves risk because we are elevating a course of action to a permanent and lasting one. We think about all the possible things that can go wrong and this starts to petrify us. There's no guarantee that the risks you take will work in your favor. That's where the calculated risk comes in and by this I mean taking action after considering the potential derailers that might come along and ways to mitigate it. The truth is that any number of things may go wrong. But an equal truth is that any number of things may go right!

Focus on Small Steps

Another suggestion to overcome risk-related fear is to look at the direction you need to take as a series of small steps, instead of one long path that you embark on without any way to change or amend your actions once you begin. Don't think of the entire task if you're feeling overwhelmed. Just think of the first step you need to take. Then take it. One step at a time and before you know it, you're well on your way.

When we take the first step in a particular direction, we can then see one step beyond where we could see from the starting point. So this extends our perspective and if, after taking an incremental step, we see that a problem may occur, then there's nothing stopping us from pivoting our perspective to move in a slightly altered direction, yet still moving toward your goals instead of away from them. And of course, there is also nothing stopping us from turning right around and returning to home base if we realize that the step we took will lead us toward problematic results. The only real way to know is to actually try and see where it takes you. And once you're comfortable with this concept and able to move forward and take calculated action, then guess what, you're on your way and before long, you will realize that you're well on your way to achieving what you set out to do.

Do Your Due Diligence

Another way to deal with risk is to try and minimize it in advance by doing due diligence. For example, when I was starting to think about resigning from a high-profile corporate job and becoming self-employed, I was aware that there were many risks that came along with that decision. But in the lead-up to the moment I had the courage to quit my job, I researched all that I could about how to set up a business and what support mechanisms were available for people who wanted to be self-employed. I also spoke to many people who had already made this transition so I could better understand some of the dynamics I would face when I made the move to self-employment myself, and how I could better prepare for the ups and downs that would come along this path. I also spoke to people in various government departments to see what resources were available to people in my situation and how to access the support available. Finally, I mitigated the risk financially by ensuring I had a cushion to fall back on in case I needed … and I did!

This same risk management process also served me well very recently when I decided to pursue my doctoral studies in my 50s. My friends thought I was a bit crazy … and sometimes so did I. But I invested the time to understand all the risks that would come along with making this choice and how to best mitigate the risks, so I would have less anxiety and enjoy the experience more.

Risk-Taking: A Short History

History is filled with examples of successful leaders who had to take risks to achieve their goals. The Wright brothers are credited with inventing the first successful powered aircraft. They made many attempts in their design and had two failed attempts at flight before they finally succeeded at Kittyhawk, NC on December 17, 1903. Fast forward to Sir Richard Branson and his company Virgin Galactic who successfully made the first manned tourist flight to suborbital space. To achieve this goal, it was necessary for about 20 years of hard work and a number of failures to successfully achieve the milestone. Elon Musk, a pioneer in the electric vehicle market started his iconic company Tesla in 2003 and has had to take many risks and endure many failures before getting to the success he enjoys today. Despite the risks he faced and continues to face even today, he believes firmly in his vision, often bucking trends and blocking out the ridicule and criticism of many disbelievers in society to stay focused on his goal and continue to pursue it one step at a time. He drew on his past experience and his previous success with PayPal, another company he successfully built and sold, and continues to do so again with his companies Starlink and SpaceX.

In my own life I've had to face my fears and the risk that comes with moving into the unknown on many occasions. The first time I recall taking a big risk was when I moved to Japan. I had just graduated, and I was hired to teach English as a foreign language in Osaka. It was my first full-time job, and I was excited, but I was also petrified because it was so far away, and I would be all alone. As I write this, I realize how funny that sounds—feeling like I would be all alone in a country with 130 million people. Yet I faced my fears and the potential risks that came along with them because the risks I took were calculated. Since then, I've continued to acknowledge risk in life and accept it. I also try and plan for it as much as possible to mitigate any negative consequences that may result. Little did I know at that time in my life how the move to Japan would prepare me for four more country moves through my career and how it would prepare me to face the risks in a more resilient way.

If At First You Don't Succeed …

When risk is involved, as it inevitably always is when living a leadership lifestyle is concerned, try not to let the risk stop you in your path. Just try and take things one step at a time and follow your plan that way. And don't forget those encouraging words in a proverb you've probably heard thousands of times through your lifetime: "If at first you don't succeed, try, try again." By doing so, you will not only move closer toward your goals, but you will be building your confidence, building your self-belief, and building your resilience in the process. These will all serve you well as you are living your leadership lifestyle. In addition, one of the greatest benefits of accepting risk as a neutral factor and taking the appropriate calculated risks when feasible is the excellent learning and growth opportunity that risk offers. By reflecting on what you experienced while taking some risk, and what you learned in the process, both about the situation and about yourself, you will be better prepared for future risks that come your way. You'll be able to make better informed decisions about what to do in those circumstances with more confidence having previously been through a situation involving some risk. This will not only give you experience but will also provide vital insight for living a leadership lifestyle.

INSIGHT 7

Build Your Resilience

When attempting to achieve any goal, there will undoubtedly be setbacks and challenges. Even with careful planning and focused action, you may not reach your goals without stubborn persistence. Persistence is another key element for living a leadership lifestyle.

In this Insight, you will find five practical steps to help you overcome hurdles without succumbing to frustration and despair—no matter how many challenges you may face on your path to the goal. These five practical steps are as follows:

1. Adopt a marathon mindset.
2. Reframe the situation when difficulty emerges.
3. Ask for help when you need it.
4. Step back every now and then to gain perspective.
5. Motivate yourself with mantras.

It's a Marathon, Not a Sprint

Overcoming challenges can take some time. That's okay. Anything truly worthwhile will require tenacity and patience. When you start to feel overwhelmed, remember that the path to success is not a sprint but a marathon. In other words, you still have plenty of time to accomplish whatever goal(s) you've set. With a marathon mindset, you won't be afraid to slow down and take stock of the situation; as in a marathon, you realize that slowing down will help you speed up again later on.

As you slow down and take stock, the important thing to remember is that all that you are facing—both challenges and victories—are an integral part of your journey to success. No matter what comes your way, if you continue to stay focused on your goal and work hard every day to move closer toward the direction of your goals, you will be a great success. Once you have slowed down, taken a breath, and given yourself the time to take stock, you can now calmly address some of the challenges and obstacles that lay before you. One way to address these challenges and obstacles in a productive and positive way is to *reframe* them.

Reframe for a Different Perspective

Reframing is a process whereby you try and see things differently to get another perspective on the situation. Often, you want to take a somewhat difficult situation or a problem and find a way to make the circumstances a bit more positive. Imagine that you are running low of funds toward the end of the month, and you're worried about having enough to cover your expenses, including groceries. You might reframe this situation by telling yourself that you're going to try and cook more creatively and utilize many seldom used ingredients you may have in your kitchen cupboards already; you make a game of it so you can stretch those funds a bit longer to take you to the end of the month. This is a situation I have known very well through different periods in my life, but the truth is that I've found the challenge of being resourceful during times of difficulty to be both stimulating and a character building as well.

Another example of reframing that helped me in life occurred when I decided to become self-employed. At first, whenever I had some down time, I used to worry about my finances, which just added to the stress of being self-employed. But as time passed and I became more comfortable with life without a salary, and all the ups and downs that go with that, I learned to reframe my down time and view it as "me time." During this me time, I could do anything I wanted, including leisure activities I once thought should only be done on weekends. And as time passed even more, I came to *love* the new-found freedom that this afforded me; even though there were some financial implications of course, I came to cherish my time and started to put a value on that so I could count my riches in different ways. This act of reframing helped me to keep going and not give up at the first sign of any obstacles on my hopes and dreams of being successfully self-employed.

Ask for Help

Something that may help you to both reframe a situation and move closer to your goals is asking for help from those who may have more knowledge or experience. It takes courage to ask for help, but the truly wise person will ask for help when needed. Don't let your pride get in the way and remember why you're asking for help … because you want to succeed and getting help might allow you to do that faster. By asking for help from others whom you trust you can see situations and problems through their eyes. Often this results in identifying something that you had not thought of yourself, but which could be very beneficial to you. Even top leaders of companies have advisors and/or executive coaches to help them make decisions, either professionally or personally.

Take a Strategic Pause When Needed

Although it may seem counterintuitive, sometimes for you move closer toward your goals, you might have to take a complete break or a pause from all related activity to gain fresh perspective. Whenever I've been faced with very difficult situations and I'm feeling at wit's end and quite helpless to do anything constructive, I've talked myself into taking a short break. Even a change of scene can help me get back on track.

Removing yourself from an environment in which you feel stuck and putting yourself in a new environment can do wonders for both your mental acuity and your physical wellness. Sometimes this may mean taking a little vacation, or perhaps this may mean something simpler to achieve like throwing yourself into a total weekend of cinematic escapism by binge watching your favorite movies (my guilty pleasure I must admit), or it could even be something simple like taking a spontaneous outing to see close family or friends with whom you have not been in contact for a while. The essential here is to stop trying so hard to "push through" or "plow ahead." This obstinance doesn't help your persistence because you are just draining your energy and spirit. Take a complete pause and you will find that more quickly than you think, you can resume with renewed energy and passion.

When I reflect on how I live my own leadership lifestyle, I realize that as a new year starts, I am filled with hopes and new goals to strive for; as the year progresses, however, life sometimes just gets a bit heavy. Despite my best efforts, I get exhausted and sometimes even too narrowly focused on achieving my goals at the expense of other things. But I'm fortunate that every year at the Christmas holidays I make a conscious decision to take a well-deserved break when I visit my family in Canada. I try as much as I can to be fully present with them. This gives me the temporary break I need and when I get back home, I'm ready to get back on track and resume my work to achieve my goals. Whatever you may choose to do during any pause you may take, be sure to try and find those things that energize you and help you to keep going when things may get a bit tough.

The Power of Personal Mantras

Another set of tools that helps me persist toward my goals are personal mantras. Personal mantras are like energy-boosting vitamins. A mantra is a thought or saying that you repeat to yourself over and over again as a self-affirmation to help you stay focused. A personal mantra can give you the motivation to help keep you going.

Mantras are often used in religious contexts but there's nothing stopping you from using a mantra to give yourself the push and encouragement to help you move forward.

I employ several different mantras, depending on the situation, to help me persist toward my goals.

For example, when I hesitate to make a decision or take action—assuming I've done a bit of due diligence and can find nothing to stop me from doing it—I use the familiar mantra, "Just go for it." I repeat this to myself quietly in my mind until I get the boost of motivation I need to move forward in that direction. When I know I'm entering a difficult or potentially stressful situation where people are sure to lose their cool, I repeat to myself "Always take the weather with you." In this case, I mean to remind myself to stay positive and have a bright and sunny demeanor, so I don't get discouraged, lose my temper, or get frustrated or angry. Sometimes my mantra can be something very simple and straightforward such as "Stay calm and sort out one thing at a time." Sometimes it's not a phrase or saying that I use; instead, I repeat some lines of some of my favorite songs—in fact I sing those lines to myself in my head—and it always puts me in a better mood and provides much needed encouragement.

Mantras can serve many purposes. For some people, their mantra may serve as an affirmation of gratitude, helping to remind them of all the good things going on in their lives. For others, mantras can help them stay focused and help to bring their vision to life through a related statement of what they want to achieve. Mantras can also be action oriented, or values based, and serve as a catalyst or code by which people live their lives.

Do you have a personal mantra? Or perhaps a favorite song from which you like a few lines of the lyrics that always seem to pick you up or make you feel better when you need it? Whatever the situation you may be facing, be it positive or negative, a personal mantra can help boost your energy and help you get through the hard work you need to in order to succeed at achieving your goals and create leadership momentum. Now that you know about the power of personal mantras, what kind of weather are you going to take with you wherever you go?

Leadership Lifestyle Exercise:
Develop Your Own Leadership Mantras

Take a moment now and create some personal mantras for yourself for each of the following situations:

- When you're feeling discouraged about something and need a pick-up.
- When you have moments of indecision, and you find it hard to take action.
- When you feel paralyzed with fear and need to get past the situation.
- When you come up against difficult challenges or obstacles that slow down your progress.
- When you must face a difficult situation, you're not looking forward to.
- When you need a boost of energy to help you carry on.
- When you succeed at something you set your mind to.

And if you're really in a mantra-making mood, once you've got your mantras for all the abovementioned situations, try thinking of some of your favorite tunes that you can use to quietly sing the mantras to in your mind for an added pick-me-up.

INSIGHT 8

Failure Is Just Opportunity in Disguise

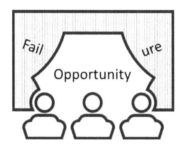

Try to turn mistakes into learning opportunities and make sure to apply your newly gained knowledge in the future. Progress happens one step at a time. Patience brings knowledge. Knowledge brings wisdom. Wisdom brings success. No matter how well you plan and no matter how hard you work, you're bound to have a few setbacks along the way. There may be times that you'll fail to accomplish what you set out to do. If you do in fact fail at some of the things you're trying to do, I want to congratulate you on experiencing one of life's most valuable lessons—failure. Nobody is perfect.

When failure occurs, people have many different ways of dealing with it. Some people are so embarrassed by the failure that they retreat for a period of time to avoid others. Other people get angry at themselves or others for failing at a task, particularly if they are quite competitive. Yet others go into a state of pure denial and make up every excuse they can think of for why they did not succeed. Regardless, there are a few important things to remember about coping with failure if you're going to achieve your goals and be a better leader.

1. Expect that significant challenges may fail.
2. Take ownership of any mistake.

3. Don't give up.

4. Don't dwell on the past.

5. Don't be your own executioner.

6. Get feedback and coaching.

Accept That Significant Challenges May Fail

If you're trying something new or more challenging than ever before, give yourself permission to fail. Failure is a necessary part of improving and bettering yourself as long as you learn from your failures. Making the same mistake repeatedly is an indication that you are not learning from your mistakes and does not lead to success.

It took me a while to learn to give myself permission to fail. Prior to that time, I was always the kind of person who wanted everything to work out just as I had planned, and actually I wanted things to turn out even better than that ... I wanted things to turn out perfectly! I pushed myself and pushed to such extremes that my health seriously suffered in the process. I was too narrowly focused on my goals that I forgot to focus on keeping myself healthy, so that I would be able to achieve my goals. I was like this with almost everything I attempted, but in the end, I learned that this was just not sustainable and if I didn't be careful, I would burn myself out in the process.

One lesson I learned about failure occurred when I submitted what I hoped would be my first published academic article. Although it had never been published in a peer-reviewed academic journal before, I expected myself to succeed even at the first attempt—partly because I had achieved many of my prior goals over the years by applying the leadership lifestyle insights written in this book.

I submitted the draft to a highly regarded top-tier academic journal for publication, filled with anticipation and hope that things would work out well. I was expecting to have to make some revisions as is usual, but I was not expecting an outright rejection with a comment that seemed to suggest I should not try again with this particular journal.

At first I was disappointed, of course. Nobody likes to fail. But then I realized what a valuable lesson this failure was and how it was a blessing in disguise. I reframed the situation into one of a learning opportunity for me, and after my discrete sulking had finished, I reflected on the comments and feedback I received. I realized I had probably submitted the draft to the wrong journal. More importantly, the experience helped me keep my ego and attitude in check and realize that I was in the middle of a learning journey, so it was ridiculous for me to think I already had all the answers.

I accepted that I had a lot more to learn, and so I gave myself permission to fail, and fail again, but only if I always took the time to learn something from the experience. I also learned that sometimes, it's okay to not be perfect, especially if your health starts to suffer. It's okay to be "good enough" and even good enough will get you far in life.

Take Ownership of Your Mistakes

Whenever you make a mistake, take ownership of that mistake. Take a step back and reflect on why you made the mistake and what you can do the next time so that you do not make that same mistake again. For example, could you have worked harder, smarter, longer to achieve your goal? Could other people have helped you, but you were too proud to ask for their help? Could you have done a better job at preparing the foundation to maximize your chances of success prior to taking any action?

You need to take ownership for your failure as much as you need to take ownership for your success. It's only by taking ownership of the bad as well as the good can we truly have influence over our own destiny and feel in control and empowered to turn things around for the better.

Don't Give Up Too Quickly

It is also very important to understand that failing at something should not be a reason to give up. It's a reason to learn and a reason to improve. Revisiting my example of failure with the article for the academic journal, I owned my failure by investing the time to truly understand what type of content is published in various journals. I reflected on whether the journals I wanted to publish in were appropriate for the kind of research I was conducting.

In searching for the answer, I spoke to colleagues in the academic world as well as mentors who are much more experienced than me to see if they could give me a steer in the right direction. I also started to communicate with the commissioning editors and other various contacts related to the journals to ask them for clarity if something was a bit vague or confusing to me. I was a bit surprised they were willing to help, and I received some great advice in the process. Another fringe benefit was that my enquiries allowed me, in a nonthreatening and nondemanding way, to introduce myself to them and start to build a rapport and establish a relationship with the journal.

Look to the Future, Don't Dwell on the Past

Being able to pick up the pieces after any failure is vitally important. Bouncing back after a challenge or difficulty is one of the most important leadership traits you can develop—and the irony is that the more you fail, the more opportunities you have to develop your resilience. How you deal with failure and pick yourself up again after falling down is telling of the kind of leader you are. Failing, learning from our failures, and then finding the resilience within yourself to bounce back after failure are crucial elements of a leadership lifestyle. To be a good leader, you must be able to be resilient and motivate yourself to stop dwelling on the failure, and to motivate yourself to move on so that you can move forward toward your success.

Don't Be Your Own Judge, Jury, and Executioner

We are often our own worst enemy because of our self-doubt in our abilities, a fear of uncertainty, a fear of failing. In many ways, although we know we shouldn't judge, we do judge ourselves because to do so is very human.

Most people tend to be their own judge and jury and never give themselves a fair chance. It might be natural to be our own judge and jury, but to live the leadership lifestyle, you must refuse to be your own executioner. Punishing yourself will serve no purpose other than to slow you down, fill you with insecurity, or worse yet, stop you in your tracks altogether because you no longer believe in the possibility of your success. Being your own executioner is destructive and offers no worthwhile value to you or anyone else. Never judge yourself too harshly. Instead, focus on the future and how you could do things differently to work around the challenges and failures you faced in the past.

Get Feedback and Coaching

Facing adversity and developing your resilience are character building to say the least, but sometimes external feedback may be the answer to helping you become a better leader and succeed at your goals. You can receive this feedback from many sources. One way to elicit feedback is to talk to trusted friends or family members whom you have no reason to doubt will be looking after your best interests. However, it may not always be appropriate for people to share their challenges with someone in their close circle of family and friends.

An alternative that many leaders use is a leadership coach. Leadership coaching is about exploration, discovery, and possibility, and achieving potential. It's a process whereby you engage in a guided journey to learn more about yourself, learn how to effectively harness your skills and capabilities, and ultimately gain forward momentum through attitude and actions that will result in the achievement of your desired goals.

To achieve this, you collaborate with the coach to create a safe space to learn about yourself and commit to deliberate and meaningful actions that serve a clearly defined purpose. This partnership is about sharing a common understanding of goals, objectives, and expectations. It's about creating a different kind of professional relationship: a coach will not solve problems for you but will help you develop the perspective and the skills to solve your own problems.

As such, the coaching relationship is unique for every person. It's based on what works for you, on what you want to achieve, and on how you want to get there. Coaches are trained to listen, observe, and be genuinely curious. Coaches seek to clarify, replaying what you say to make sure you're effectively communicating, and encouraging you to pinpoint what is truly important. Coaching is all about learning and discovery—uncovering what motivates and inspires you, identifying your key values and beliefs, finding out what gets you stuck and helping you to break through barriers and overcome the challenges you face. Most importantly, coaching is all about taking accountability for your own success. You do this by applying the tools and insights you learn through the coaching process and taking thoughtful and considered action to achieve your goals and understand how to measure your progress. Coaching will help determine what success looks like and what you need to do to get to where you want to be.

A coach will help you see new possibilities and help you become the leader you want to be. Leadership coaching is about developing, utilizing, maintaining, and improving a set of skills and capabilities that enable you to achieve goals through focused and deliberate actions and with intent, influence, and purpose. More importantly, leadership is a way of life, a chosen lifestyle if you will, that contributes to your professional and personal success regardless of the circumstances you face.

No matter where you choose to get your feedback, be open to the different perspective you'll hear about your situation, the insights that you may receive from hearing a different viewpoint on what you may be facing, and the coaching you receive that may help you see new possibilities to achieve your goals and get unstuck so you can move forward confidently.

I benefited a great deal from leadership coaching through my professional and personal life. I believe in it so much, that I studied, trained, and qualified as a coach myself by earning a Master of Coaching degree a few years ago. Since then, I've coached many senior executives and mid-level professionals striving to get ahead in their working lives, and I've also coached many younger aspirational leaders working on earning advanced degrees. No matter who I'm coaching, the patterns seem to be the same. People don't realize that all they need to achieve whatever they aspire to is within their grasp already just by having a growth mindset and taking ownership for their failures and their successes and by living a leadership lifestyle.

Often, the early coaching work is about helping people to acknowledge and accept the situation they are in, and then let go of the victim mindset and harness their inner potential so they can thrive. Once this is realized, the positive momentum takes over and propels them toward their goals. And the best part about it is they become aware of their own abilities in a way that was somehow clouded before. Onward and upward ... the world is their oyster!

Let me give you an example from some coaching work I recently did with a client. Some of the details have been changed for confidentiality reasons, but the core lesson remains the same. Andrew was trying for many years to earn a promotion but had failed to achieve this several times in the past. He became fixated on trying to show everyone around him that he deserved the promotion and struggled to contain the embarrassment every time he was not successful. Through the coaching work we did together, he came to realize what his true value proposition was to his firm, and more importantly how his values were strongly aligned to the company he worked for, which he did not want to leave to seek a higher position elsewhere. Through the coaching work, he learned how to reframe his failure, both for himself and in how he positioned himself for future promotions, by communicating why he was right for the promotion instead of overly focusing on what he could do. He started to speak about the impact his work has had on others and how this would be even more beneficial if his role and position were elevated at the next round of promotions. He learned to transform the way he articulated his pitch from what he could do to why he was the right person to promote. Before long, his new approach gained some traction, and he was successfully promoted the following year. His failure at first, although understandably disappointing and frustrating, turned into a key learning and growing experience for him as he took ownership of his failure and was open to coaching to help him break through previous barriers to his success. Failure truly is just an opportunity in disguise ... so long as you learn from it and be open to where it can lead you, with a little bit of help every now and then.

INSIGHT 9

Be Courageous and
Carve Your Own Path

Living a leadership lifestyle means resisting the temptation to blindly follow others. In today's world, it's so easy to get caught up in the noise of everyday life and society. We are constantly inundated by the prolific social media messages that try and dictate how we should live our lives, what we should look like, how we should dress, what we should or shouldn't eat, who we should be friends with, and what we should avoid.

These opinions are filtered through the lens of people who seem popular to the masses and who we believe we should emulate in order to get the same benefits of fame and fortune that modern society makes us feel is important; and if we don't achieve these things, then our own lives amount to nothing. This is a toxic aspiration that has an adverse impact on society. And shown by the history of the truly important problems of our time that affect everyone, such as climate change, social justice, and equality, leaders in the making are at the forefront of pushing back against society's pressures to follow the crowd. Through their example, leaders show that blindly following the path that others tell you to take is not a way to live a leadership lifestyle, but instead the way to live the lifestyle of a follower.

In one of my leadership roles, I thought I had finally "arrived" at my forever (professional) home. I was put in charge of a flourishing business that continuously performed well in a company that was strongly aligned to my core values. Yet as time went by, I found I was not fulfilled despite everything going for me. I felt like it was déjà vu, having had a similar experience of discontent when I worked in Monaco some years earlier. At first, I tried to shrug this off and just pretend as if everything was going to be okay. But as time progressed, the feelings of unhappiness just went from bad to worse. Once again in my life I had to do some significant soul searching, which as you get older and more established becomes more and more difficult; your insights tell you that you need to move in a different direction, but you hesitate to undertake another change yet again. There is so much pressure, some self-imposed and some imposed by others, to just stay the course in hopes that things will get better.

However, having been in this position at several points in my life, I've learned that the most important thing you can do to live a leadership lifestyle is to be true to yourself because the situation rarely gets better. Instead, you just end up blaming and getting angry at yourself for not acting sooner—even though the decisions you have to make may not be understood by others and may even be very unpopular and take you down a more challenging path. This was the situation I was in as I decided to resign from an incredible professional role that many people coveted and move abroad again to a place where I felt I was more at home.

Colleagues and friends thought I was a bit crazy and impulsive when I shared this decision, not realizing how much thinking and planning had led to this decision. At first, I found it hard and lonely as I didn't feel supported by those from whom I expected support. But eventually I realized that I did not need others to understand my decision and the actions taken. I just needed them to accept and respect my decision and my awareness of what was the right thing for me to do for myself at the time.

This lonely path resulted in many challenges and difficulties, but I did not have any regrets. I had anticipated some of the difficulties I experienced and planned the best I could to deal with them. Of course, there were other challenges I had no way of anticipating whatsoever and for these, I just had to cross those bridges as they came along and deal with them the best I could in the moment. Sometimes I managed to circumvent the challenges; at other times, I had to accept that this was a consequence of the decisions I made and the actions I took, and then I had to take ownership and accountability of the circumstances I was in, and not let a victim mindset creep in. But many silver linings and amazing opportunities also presented themselves to me because of this path I had taken. Although I struggled to find employment in the months after I moved abroad, I ended up setting up my own business and doing work that genuinely aligned with who I was at my core. At first things started out slowly, but in time things picked up and although one can never predict that things will always go well, I have learned how to deal with ambiguity more effectively and developed my own leadership resilience through the process. This path also opened the door for me to pursue one of my personal passions, lifelong learning. Because of my new circumstances, I was able to find a truly transformational learning program that helped me develop both personally and professionally and take my own skills and abilities to a higher level. In time this resulted in some wonderful and unique new opportunities personally, not to mention the great new relationships I established along the way and paved the way for new and even better professional opportunities to come along. Let me share a bit more about what was going on in my life at that time.

I was repatriated back to Canada to work in a large financial services organization. I was responsible for managing a team that looked after one of the company's key customer groups and my team had consistently been the profitability driver of the business across the country. Things were going well for a while, but after about two years or so, the situation started to deteriorate and I started to think more and more that perhaps this was not the place I once thought it was, and perhaps this is not the place for me. With this awareness I started to see more of the negative around me and after a while, I knew what I had to do, and I also knew it was not going to be easy. Eventually, I made the move back to the United Kingdom and tried to get re-established once again. Like the first time around when I moved to the United Kingdom, things were difficult for a while, but having had my previous experience I had confidence I would get through the difficult times and land on my feet. I was hoping to find work in the financial services sector again, but I also stayed open minded about what my next steps could be. I promised myself that I was going to prioritize work that aligned more with my core values and provided a meaningful purpose for me. After some time passed, I started doing some leadership coaching work and found I truly enjoyed it. It was very sporadic work, but I got excited at the thought of creating something new and worthwhile and something I felt was truly about connecting with people and helping others. Eventually I set up a leadership coaching business, which I was very enthusiastic and hopeful about. But my passion for lifelong learning was also niggling at the back of my mind and I wanted to continue my learning in some relevant way. I found a wonderful course that seemed to call to me through the screen of my computer. It was an Executive Master of Consulting and Coaching for Change degree that was being offered at a highly respected business school in France. It was a truly transformation course for me, both personally and professionally and I'm so glad I had the courage and initiate to pursue one of my passions. But my income was very unpredictable, and the cost of the program was quite prohibitive. I seriously thought about not going, but then I thought about all the ups and downs in my life and all the little setback I've had before, and I made the commitment to myself that I was going to do it and would make the adjustments to my life that were necessary to achieve this objective. Those in my close circle of friends found it a bit difficult at first to understand why I wanted to study again; they did not seem on side, especially because of the financial burden and added stress this brought into my life. But once I started, they soon realized how important this was for both my personal growth and my professional development. And I now have some lifelong friends through that program who have shared a very significant transitional time in my life and a truly transformational experience for all of us.

This Insight shows that you can develop the courage to journey down the paths less traveled if you:

1. Choose the path *you* want to take.
2. Don't look back.
3. Enjoy the wonder, learn from the challenges.
4. Check your inner compass.
5. Prepare to be courageous.

Choose the Path *You* Want to Take

Take a moment to reflect on your own situation. Whose journey are you on: yours or someone else's? To live a leadership lifestyle, it's important that you have clarity about this question because it can be very easy to get off track and lose your way. Try and think hard about your own journey to leadership and how it may differ from someone else's. What are the things that may be unique to you, or specific to your circumstances that all the other voices out there may not have to consider?

By reflecting on these things, you can start to differentiate your journey from those of other people. The biggest benefit of such reflection is an internal calm and sense of individuality that will help you sift through all the external noise in the world so you can more effectively focus on your own path to leadership. If we think back to Insight 1 (You Are Responsible for Your Own Success) you start to realize and understand that the path you should follow is defined by you and unique to you.

In the process of trying to determine your own path, it is natural that we want to share our thoughts or perhaps bounce ideas off our closest friends and even family members. But not everyone will understand what motivates you in the same way that you will understand yourself. For many people it may be hard to comprehend why someone may want to go against the norm and follow their individual path instead of the safer, easier, and more established road ahead that most people will journey on. The result is subtle or latent peer pressure or groupthink whereby people try and talk you into taking the route that everyone else takes. This often comes from a place of love and support, so try not to misinterpret their intentions. However, from time to time this also may come from a place of jealousy, fear, and possibly even envy as they know deep down that they don't have the courage or initiative, perhaps, to take that path themselves. Try not to let this pressure be an anchor weighing you down or holding you back. Because if you become clear on your path and then don't follow it, you will always regret it and will forever be asking yourself what would have happened if you had taken that road less traveled instead of playing it safe.

A good friend of mine had a real talent for music. Studying music energized him and more importantly, gave him a great deal of pleasure.

But because of the circumstances he was in, he was pressured to study more business and scientific disciplines as these, he was told by others, would be safer, get him established better in life, and offer him more stability in the long term. There were many times I could see him battling internally with this dilemma. He wanted to pursue what he loved, a career in music would have made him so much happier, but the messages and feedback he received from others scared him into thinking he should do what was expected to lead a stable and secure life. Although he tried to pursue music on the side, having to hold down a full-time job that at times became very stressful and required very long hours would not allow for this to be done very successfully. Over time he became more and more disillusioned, and slipped into a mild depression, being full of regret for not carving out his own path, but simply following the path suggested by others.

One of the outcomes of the Covid-19 pandemic is a phenomenon being referred to as "The Great Resignation" where thousands of people are quitting their jobs because they are unhappy doing what they do. I've also heard this being referred to as "the great rethink," "the great restart," "the great regroup," and "the great reset." Whatever you want to call it, they are all very similar and have a lot to do with people making choices that are more suitable for them. The constraints of the pandemic have given people the time to realize that they should try to pursue professional goals that are more aligned with their purpose and their core values.

Keep Looking Forward

Once you accept and embed deeply in your mind the idea that you have to follow your own path, you may come to the realization that your own path may be very different from anyone else you know. Sometimes this realization is accompanied with a feeling of liberation and excitement; however, this realization can also be accompanied with an overwhelming feeling of loneliness and fear. You start to understand that there are no templates or magic formulas to follow and guide you and that you may have to feel your way through your journey without a map of any sort.

The lucky among us will stumble upon some great people who can act as temporary guides or mentors along our journey, but ultimately, it's up to each person to take the steps along their own path in order to make any progress. And even if you do find helpful travelers along your journey, you may soon start to realize that you may be embarking on a journey that takes you on the road less traveled, and this can be scary. I sometimes wonder what would have happened if I had stayed in that leadership role at that company and just hoped that things would get better. Would I have progressed further up the senior ranks? Would I be more successful, whatever that means? I know I definitely would be more financially well off, but would this automatically translate into increased happiness?

When I get into this mode of thinking about what could have been, I quickly remind myself that nobody has a crystal ball that can tell the future, so there's no point in dwelling on it and wasting mental energy on hypotheticals from situations in the past. Of course, it's important to reflect and learn from the past, but don't get stuck regretting or resenting what happened in the past. Let it go and refocus on what you may have learned from past experiences and how you'll apply those insights to your future. Remember Insight 6 (Accept That Risk is Part of Living a Leadership Lifestyle)? Being courageous and carving your own path is a perfect example of how you may have to embrace risk and learn to live with it in order to live your leadership lifestyle.

Enjoy the Wonder, Learn From the Challenges

Although it's human nature and sometimes easier to focus on the negative, it's worthwhile and helpful to keep in mind that the road less traveled is often full of unexpectedly wondrous things, most often the kind of things that help us have new experiences that help us to grow in all aspects of our life. For example, we may face challenges and obstacles along the way that test our character and expand our preconceived personal boundaries in a way we would have never imagined nor conceived had we not started down our individual path. The result is a renewed sense of self and increased confidence on what we are capable of despite having obstacles in our way.

Carving our own path may also require us to learn new skills and increase the set of capabilities that will help us during the course of our life, and also allow us to help others who may need our help from time to time. The other benefit, not to be overlooked, of taking the road less traveled is that we encounter a whole new group of people whom we may never have met had we not taken this path. The rich and robust diversity of personalities, experiences, lifestyles, ideas, friendships, and stories we are exposed to can also be beneficial, as we have an opportunity to learn and grow exponentially through the eyes of others whom we meet along the way. Of course, this means that we may have to go out of our own comfort zones and engage with them to meet them, get to know them, learn from them, and also share our own stories all the while being open minded to both the similarities and differences that may emerge.

When I graduated with my bachelor degree and completed some follow-up studies the following year, I found myself in a situation where I was not able to land a job. The economy was bad that year, and I recall being a bit scared at the time. I had amassed a great deal of student debt and it was important for me to be a good citizen and a contributing member of society. One of my classmates at the time had told me she was going to teach English in Japan and I was intrigued so I asked more questions and found myself exploring this path—one that I had never aspired to nor anticipated in my life. Later that year I was hired by a language company to teach English in Osaka, Japan, and before I knew it, I was on the plane on my way to Japan. I remember vividly the flight to Japan, sitting in my seat, petrified. I did not know anyone in Japan, I only knew three words in Japanese (hello, goodbye, and thank you) and I had never been trained as a teacher, nor had even aspired to being a teacher. And this was the first full-time job I had ever held, adding to my anxiety. Yet I had this great opportunity to do something that most people don't get the chance to do. It was difficult at first, and indeed all the way through my time there. I struggled with the language ... often. I struggled with loneliness and feeling like I had no support network. I struggled with the distance from close family members and good friend. At one point, I even found myself in a life-threatening situation when a devastating earthquake hit Japan.

I overcame all these obstacles by having a positive attitude, an open mindset, and courage as my companion. As a result, the experience brought wonders into my life that I could never have anticipated. In time I became more proficient speaking conversational Japanese. I was introduced to delicious and artistic food (including food I would never have imagined eating, such as jellyfish … for the record, it was a one-time thing only). Most importantly, I made some amazing lifelong friends with whom I still keep in touch despite the 30 years that have passed since my time there.

Taking that road less traveled at the beginning of my working life helped shape my views and perspectives in a way that remains with me to this day. Through the first-hand experience of a foreign culture, I had the chance to see the world through different lenses. This experience also helped me develop valuable life skills that I still put into practice every day of my life.

If you're on the road less traveled as you try to live your leadership lifestyle, you may find that it's much broader, more winding, and harder to see around corners than if you had taken the straight and narrow path. It also means that there will be fewer road signs and guideposts to help you find your way. You may have to explore paths that may lead to obstacles or a dead-end that require you to turn around. If you have to change course, as anyone who chooses different paths will, don't become frustrated or discouraged—or judge yourself negatively for making a mistake … after all, how were you supposed to know that the trail would lead to an obstacle or a dead end. The only way you could find out is by going down the trail, and by doing so you have acquired new knowledge that will help you in the future to avoid the traps and mistakes that ensnared you the first time.

Obstacles help you prepare mentally and emotionally for what may come, and this preparation will develop over time into a kind of resilience that will allow you to face these kinds of challenges and adversity more effectively. You also learn how to think creatively to circumvent the challenges and obstacles in your way and so you can continue down your chosen path.

By now it's probably becoming clear to you that carving your own path may not be easy and almost certainly will not be straightforward. If you've ever taken a journey before and gotten lost, you may have been able to check a map to help get you back on track. But as you try living your leadership lifestyle, you may find the types of maps required are difficult and sometimes even impossible to find.

But expecting this situation to happen from time to time and planning ahead for when it may happen can be significantly helpful. As I started my doctoral studies—clearly the road less traveled for someone in their 50s—I found myself experiencing angst on a regular basis as this current aspiration is unlike anything I'd ever done before. There was so much ambiguity and lack of clarity that I oftentimes felt quite lonely; my closest friends had taken different paths in their lives.

My life experience however had taught me and given me confidence to believe I could manage through the twists and turns that this new endeavor brought my way. When I felt myself sinking into an anxiety pit, I took a deep breath and reminded myself of all the different experiences I've had and different roads I've been on, each with their own unique challenges, some of which had been much more difficult than the challenges of pursuing my doctorate. Yet I managed to make it through those situations, sometimes with a few metaphoric bumps and bruises to remind me of the challenges I faced, but more often making it through those situations and coming out a stronger and more resilient person.

Although I didn't have a clear and concise map to help me navigate the new situation, I had faith and confidence that I would make it through.

Check Your Inner Compass

Always remember to take time along your journey to check your inner compass to ensure you're still on your chosen path. Any journey will be filled with unexpected twists and turns that can lead you to discover scenic wonders; however, these twists and turns also sometimes be distracting and seductively lead us astray. Therefore, it's important that you regularly take time to check in with yourself and reflect on your journey so far. Are you still on the path you initially wanted to take? If not, why has this happened? Where on the path did you start to go astray? Perhaps it's okay that you've been diverted from your initial path to a new one that may have taken you on a tangent or parallel path. However, if you want to return to the initial path, what is needed or what will help you to get back on track?

When you're trying to live a leadership lifestyle, one of the most important things to help you succeed is to check in with yourself periodically to ensure you are where you want to be.

Prepare to Be Courageous

Carving your own path can be the most amazing and rewarding step you take, but it is not for the faint-hearted. There may be challenges and obstacles around every corner that test your character and the very fabric of your being. So, if you decide that you want to carve your own path, take some time before you start to think about the role that courage will play on the journey. You will need to demonstrate courage more often than you might initially expect and in many different forms. Courage may be needed emotionally, mentally, physically, and financially, and there may be times when you just feel like giving up and turning around and going back to the place you started. If these situations occur, remind yourself just how far you've already come, how much you've already learned, how much you've grown, and how many challenges you've overcome just to get where you are now.

And remind yourself that every step further that you take brings you one step closer to where you are going and takes you one step farther away from where you started. Eventually, that road less traveled will lead you to a new place and your journey on the road less traveled will have earned you new strength, new experiences, new relationships, new confidence, new insights, and new perspectives, all of which are necessary, on a continuous basis, for living a leadership lifestyle.

When I first moved to the United Kingdom in 2003, I had no job lined up but many possibilities in the pipeline. Shortly after I arrived, the war in Iraq had broken out, and I found myself struggling financially because companies in my field were very conservative and were not hiring during that time. I interviewed for many roles and eventually received an offer for a job after a few months. Despite needing to find work, I declined this job because the role was not right for me when I assessed it against my genuine identity profile (Insight 2). As a result, the following months were difficult for me as I struggled to keep afloat financially. I often thought that I should have just accepted that job, which would have allowed me to continue to look for a more appropriate role without having the intense financial pressure. But to take a job with no intention of staying was not my personal brand; I could not act with this kind of ill will and deception, so I continued my search.

There were many dark moments when I repeatedly questioned the path I was on and in the darkest of times, I even found myself starting to plan an exit strategy and return to Canada. But I persevered and exhausted every possibility trying to stay true to myself, demonstrating personal courage, and a steadfast belief in myself and my abilities. Eventually, I landed a role that was right for me working for a youth development charity as a senior fund raising professional, and after a few more months had passed my situation stabilized. Had I given up and not had the courage to stay the course, my life would have taken a different turn and certainly would not have had the wealth of opportunity that came my way in unique experiences, in new skills development, and in new and meaningful relationships that emerged from this first job in the United Kingdom.

The great poet Ralph Waldo Emerson once wrote, "Do not go where the path may lead, go instead where there is no path and leave a trail." These words, which I first heard many years ago, have stuck with me throughout my life and still stay with me today. When necessary, I have always sought advice and guidance from others and listened to what they have to say, but I always compliment their feedback with my own inner compass and the path I believe I should be on. This has led me to amazing places and experiences throughout my life. When I reflect on how I carved my own path, it has become clear to me that courage was my constant traveling companion on my road less traveled, although I had not known it at the time.

Courage was my companion when I decided to move to Japan in my early 20s and work in a foreign country and culture that I had never been exposed to before. Courage was also my companion when I chose to leave some well-paying jobs in banking, not once, but twice in my career. Leaving my banking job the first time led to an amazing life experience of being part of a team that brought Pope John Paul II to Toronto in 2002; this experience, in turn, led me to move to the United Kingdom in 2003 to spread my wings and broaden my professional horizons while challenging myself. The second time I left a good banking job occurred in 2015 when I resigned from the seemingly perfect executive job that was just not fulfilling to me.

These experiences have collectively helped me to better think critically, taking multiple perspectives into account, think about issues of diversity and inclusion, especially when dealing with culturally sensitive situations, be a more effective and empathetic communicator to bring people along the ride with me and get their buy in, and think more strategically and plan as best as possible for unanticipated and unwanted occurrences. Most importantly, these experiences have helped shape my own perspectives on leadership as a conscious choice we make to live a leadership lifestyle in the most constructive way possible.

This theme of courage has been present in my life in so many ways and at so many times. Courage is needed when you want to move forward in a direction that will knowingly bring challenge and difficulty your way, be it financial, psychological, or creating challenging circumstances ... and sometimes all three at once. This was the case with some of my higher education pursuits in mid-life, which, some could argue, are indulgences in my life at this stage.

No one may be able to understand why I make some of the choices that I do, but that's okay. They don't need to understand. They just need to accept that I am carving my own path, and courage is helping me every step of the way. When faced with making decisions that require me to carve my own path repeatedly, I don't think about the hardships that may come along the journey and the problems that I may face. Instead, I remember the many times I've had to carve my own path before, and I take comfort in the knowledge that I've found my way through the storms each time. And because of those experiences, I've developed the confidence to face the unknown again and again, all the while knowing that I'm traveling the road that I am meant to be on. Courage has been and continues to be my constant companion as I continue every day to live my own leadership lifestyle.

Leadership Lifestyle Exercise: Carving Your Own Path

Take a moment now and reflect on the following situations that you may encounter as you carve your own path:

1. What does your own path look like?
2. What scenic points do you expect along the way?
3. What preparation will you make so you can deal with peer pressure and group think?
4. Are you traveling alone, or can you identify other who can act as temporary guides and mentors to accompany you on some parts of your journey?
5. What tools can you use to break through difficult boundaries and barriers that you come across (e.g., mantras)?
6. How can you recognize the difference between a temporarily closed road and a dead end?
7. How can you navigate a closed road if obstacles are in the way?
8. How can you prepare for dealing with dead ends if that's where you find yourself from time to time?
9. How will you check your inner compass to ensure you're still on your chosen path?
10. How will you leave a trail for others to follow?

INSIGHT 10

You Define Progress and Success

The messages we receive from the world around us can be deceptive and limiting. Sometimes it becomes a matter of information overload that makes us think and feel that the most prolific and dominant messages we hear equate to the simple truth. But this is not always the case.

Living a leadership lifestyle means understanding that there is *no one truth nor one way* of doing things that will be right for everyone. In this Insight, I apply the recognition of different truths for different people to the concepts of progress and success. The following lessons will help you achieve progress and success on your own terms:

1. Align your definition of success with who you are.
2. Be open to nonlinear progress.
3. Let go of the past.
4. Don't let anticipation overwhelm reality.
5. Use mental images to capture what success means to you.
6. Enjoy the journey.

Align Your Definition of Success With Who You Are

In the context of what it means to be successful, most people are happy to follow the established convention in society that success means continuously moving forward along a linear plane that takes you higher and higher, climbing the ladder as it's known, and eternally striving for that which is so high that it sometimes feels unreachable. We have come to use this paradigm when we evaluate or judge our own success, breaking the construct down into items that seemingly help us measure our progress such as job titles, income levels, and overall wealth. But these are in a way limited and limiting manifestations of success and in some cases difficult for many people to attain. Does missing these commonly accepted markers of achievement mean there has been no progress, and hence, no success? The answer is a resounding "NO."

It's important to be open to new experiences, even if you did not plan them, and it's critical that you create your own definitions of progress and success—definitions that reflect your genuine identity and consider your values, key motivators, and personal drivers. If you stop to think about what success means to you, you may find that that it has nothing to do with financial gain or job titles or power. Of course, those things are important to some extent, but they don't define you and they don't guarantee your success. There are many high-powered and highly paid individuals who feel empty inside. Despite the high level of wealth, authority, and power they may have acquired in certain environments, they are still filled with a gaping void inside. They do not feel as if they are progressing or they are successful because authority, power, and wealth are inconsistent with their authentic, internal definition of what progress and success mean to them.

If you're living a leadership lifestyle, progress and success may not always be monetary. These are actually very intangible concepts, but society makes people feel like monetary gain is the only manifestation of progress and success. But the concepts are sometimes at odds with each other. Sit down and reflect on what success means to you. Then try to write down a definition of success that you can keep in your mind constantly and remind yourself when needed; you may find that financial gain is quite detached from what progress and success truly mean to you. This won't be the case for everyone. Our definitions of progress and success are a product of the environmental conditions that influence us, and our own unique perspectives and willingness to look deep within to come up with our own definitions. Regardless, everyone's unique definitions may take them to places they had not imagined nor considered before.

Be Open to Nonlinear Progress

If you remain open-minded about what progress and success mean to you, you may end up in some interesting places that can help you grow as a leader in unimaginable ways. For some people, it may even result in what from the outside looks like *backward* motion; in reality, this is far from the case. You won't be moving backward at all because you are consciously making a choice to move in a direction that gives you forward momentum in your life, despite what a job title or income level may suggest.

And you will gain intangible assets that very often get discounted in traditional definitions of progress and success. For example, you may have some profoundly personal and/or professional developmental experiences: you may learn new skills or languages; you may gain insights into new work cultures that will help you in your future career; you will meet new people and establish new personal and professional relationships that allow you to have better and broader perspective while expanding your own mindsets and previous boundaries; and you will amass a repertoire of new and exciting stories that will help you relate to others beyond your own homogeneous circles and benefit from the richness of diversity in all its existing and emerging forms.

Not everyone will want to give up the traditional definitions of success, including linear advancement and monetary reward. As human beings, we all have an incredible ability to adapt, but it's easier for some people than others. Some people are less flexible than others, and find safety in the known, while experiencing more fear and anxiety when it comes to the unknown. This is not to say that one way is right, and another way is wrong; indeed both traditional and nontraditional definitions of success are valid. People are different and we must all respect each other's differences even if their choices would not work for us.

Let Go of the Past

In order to live a leadership lifestyle, you will regularly be required to "let go" of the past and embrace the new and emerging. Letting go does not mean forgetting, in fact quite the opposite. Letting go means remembering how it was, what you gained, what you learned, and reflecting on how you can use those valuable lessons to continue living your leadership lifestyle as the new and unknown enter your life. For some this may mean assuming new roles that don't come with a fancy, powerful job title—and may even result in lower income and financial loss. As long as you take the time to understand what progress means to you, such as learning new skills and having new experiences, and you factor these measures of progress into your authentic definition of success, you will soon realize that living a leadership lifestyle means understanding and embracing that progress is not linear and success is not always monetary.

Don't Let Anticipation Overwhelm Reality

One of the insights I've gained through my work as a leadership coach is that most people are often more afraid at the *thought* of what may have to be sacrificed rather than the actual reality of having to give something up. That anticipation of the unknown creates a high level of fear and resistance to change. When the actual change actually occurs, my clients often surprise themselves at how easily they were able to adapt and how little the change impacted their lives. Of course, this is not the case with all change. Some types of change may have a material impact on people's lives. One example is when a reduction in income necessitates lifestyle changes. Nevertheless, adapting to change, positive or negative, can often be easier than we anticipate.

Use Mental Images to Capture
What Success Means to You

When I think about progress and success in the context of my own life, I often remember the song by the Beatles called "The Long and Winding Road." The lyrics of the song actually don't have much to do with my reflection, but rather the title of the song evokes an image in my mind that brings comfort to me when I feel like I'm stuck and not making any progress at all. I have reached a point in my life where I seldom think of my own success as a destination, but rather as a series of growth experiences along the individual path I have carved for myself. I measure my progress and success by the ability to find new ways to challenge and develop myself in order to reach my human potential. This definition is often accompanied by several psychological/mental associations.

The first is the image of a winding road going up and down a series of tall mountains. The only way I have to travel from my starting point to where I want to end up is by going up the winding road on one side of the first mountain and then down the winding road on the other side of that mountain. Then I have to repeat the sequence until I am able to get across the entire mountain range.

Another image I have often in relation to progress and success is of the optical illusion known as the Penrose Stairs. It's a set of stairs in a square shape that seems to have no starting point and no ending point, and this is the same regardless of if you're going up or down the stairs.

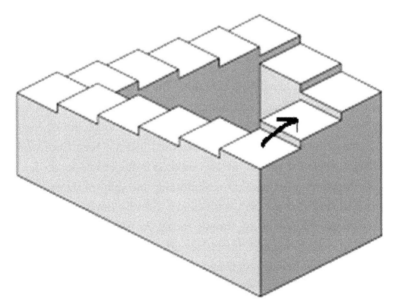

Penrose Stairs Model.
Start at the square closest to you and go upward in
a counterclockwise direction.

At first, the Penrose Stairs image might seem like an argument against progress of any kind since you always end up where you've already been. But every time you go around you are learning new things, gaining new information, and seeing things from different perspectives, as well as applying knowledge you picked up on the last trip around. So, although it might seem like you're right back where you started, in reality you've gained so much in the process and are much further ahead than when you began. My takeaway from this is not to worry about getting somewhere (i.e., a destination), and just enjoy the walking on the stairs.

A different yet similar image of this can also be something like a winding corkscrew, the kind that is used to open wine bottles. If you hold the corkscrew up and imagine yourself starting at the pointed tip and then walking upward around the winding part, you will seem to come back to the same place many times. What's different, however, is that you may be in the same place, but you'll be at a higher level. Your perspective will be similar, yet different as the further up you go the further beyond along the horizon, you'll be able to see, and every time you arrive at the same position, but at a higher level, you see things with the previous wisdom you've gained when you were at that same spot the time before.

Enjoy the Journey

You have probably heard the expression, "The journey is much better than the destination." When I was younger, I had a difficult time understanding what this meant. It was because I had not had enough life experience to relate to the expression and also because I had not been faced with a situation where the path of my own progress in life was no longer linear. I only began to understand the true meaning and value of the expression once I realized that my path was taking a different direction from most other people I knew in my various circles. At first it was quite unsettling, but once I became comfortable with my nonlinear path and both accepted and embraced nonfinancial measures of my success, only then did the true wealth and benefits of experience and opportunity become apparent to me. In time, these benefits have become crystal clear as they have helped me achieve things I had not thought possible and never would have even attempted had I not had a winding road to travel on.

Two instances in particular stand out for me in regard to making nonlinear progress toward success. The first was making the decision to work in the charitable sector instead of continuing in the commercial sector where I was most comfortable. This decision came with a great deal of financial sacrifice as I earned only about one-third of what I was earning in my previous corporate role. However, the richness it brought into my life is impossible to measure. I met a totally different set of people and gained insights into a different culture. The interesting characters along the way double as protagonists who enrich the many stories of my travels and life that I share with others. One of these people was a manager of mine who I really admired; however, when I think back, I don't think I ever told him so at the time. Because of the nature of the work we were doing, things often got a bit chaotic when we had to go into "production mode." But whenever the situation got stressful, he would always just stop whatever he was doing, ground himself for a moment, take a long, deep breath, and then very calmly say in a deep and loud voice, "It will all be okay." I found this most interesting because in all the roles I had before, and all the roles I've had since then, I had never met anyone else who coped with stressful situations in that way. It made such an impression on me that I now do that myself, although I say the words in my mind and not out loud. I even tell this story to other people when I sense or can see that they are getting stressed. It helps to break the tension and puts a smile on their faces. They say that emulation is the best form of flattery, and I'm so pleased I had the chance to work with that manager as I've carried a little bit of him along throughout my life since then.

Making the sacrifice to go into the charitable sector may have seemed like a backward step. Ultimately, however, that decision led me back to the commercial sector with a new professional identity that continued to expand my horizons and led me to places and experiences that might never had occurred. What comes to mind as I write this is being head hunted to work in wealth management directly from a charitable role. Because of the relationship I had built with ultrahigh net worth individuals, and the comfort and poise with which I was able to interact with members of this community, I was an ideal candidate to join a private banking business. I knew that the bank that hired me was probably most interested in my contacts and the relationships I had established, but my first big success as a private banker did not come through that. I worked hard and utilized all my resourcefulness and transferable skills, which I learned while working in the charitable sector, and that was what earned me a new key client that got the attention of management. This eventually led to a relocation to Monaco, which for me, was like a dream coming true as I had wanted to live there since the first time I visited while backpacking as a university student. That seemingly backward move was in fact a great enabler of progress in my life.

The second experience that resonates in relation to this chapter is the decision to become self-employed. My income level went from high to zero from one day to the next and although the experience was accompanied with a great deal of fear and anxiety, I continued to hang on to my nonfinancial measures of progress and success to get me through some of the many difficult and darkest times along my journey.

When I look back now and reflect on the nonlinear progress in my life, and then on the resulting success it has brought my way, I am both humbled and amazed at the nonfinancial benefits and riches that have come my way, the most important of which has been an incredible sense of personal growth and accomplishment resulting in confidence, resilience, and a healthy dose of discreet personal pride.

Take a moment now to reflect on what progress and success mean to you and how you will measure your own progress and success along the way.

INSIGHT 11

Celebrate the Successes Along the Way

Sometimes when you set your mind to something, it's easy to get overly focused on achieving your goals. When this happens, there is a chance that you try so hard to stay on track that you become blind to the little wins along the way that are, in essence, steppingstones to success along your journey. The following will help you stay mindful of your progress, which will motivate you to keep moving forward:

1. Don't push yourself to excess.
2. Celebrate the successes.
3. Practice mindfulness.
4. Learn to identify successes.
5. Keep an achievement journal.
6. Don't let achievements fade in importance.
7. Celebrate with others.
8. Celebrate the personal successes of others.

Don't Push Yourself to Excess

Obsessive perfectionism is unproductive and unhealthy both physically and psychologically. You can be trying so hard to achieve something that, over time, your physical health deteriorates because you are pushing yourself beyond what may be healthy for you. Psychologically speaking, you may be working so hard toward something that you get mentally exhausted, which can result in a diminished ability to cope with the emotional ups and downs along your winding path. Even worse, the physical and psychological exhaustion that may come about through a sustained period of trying too hard may lead you to descend into a vicious cycle of discouragement and decreased motivation to carry on.

This dynamic can be seen in many different situations. Athletes try and excel in their chosen sport but sometimes train so hard that they damage their physical health and burn out prematurely. Students studying for exams revise so much that the mental exhaustion from overpreparing actually makes them perform worse in their exams. Employees in many companies are constantly trying to do more and better in order to be acknowledged and perhaps recognized and positioned for promotion. Don't get me wrong, trying to improve yourself to achieve your full potential is something to be admired and encouraged. But when taken to the extreme in an unhealthy way, pushing too hard can actually do a great deal of damage and this should be avoided as much as possible.

Another detriment that often occurs when you get overly focused on something in an unhealthy way is that you can start to lose the joy of being on the journey. What once started out as an exciting adventure for you, enabled by your passion, turns into an exhausting chore that becomes a demotivating and discouraging journey through hell. You start to view your work as unfulfilling and lose sight of why you even wanted to travel along this path in the first place. Eventually, things become so bad that you give up. The antidote to putting relentless pressure on yourself is to try and stop often along the journey to *be present* and acknowledge the little achievements you've accomplished. Each achievement is a step forward on your leadership path.

Celebrate the Big and Small Successes

Living a leadership lifestyle means acknowledging, understanding, and accepting that there will be times in your life that you may not realize that you are making progress, so you have to remind yourself of just how much you have achieved so far. It's an important and helpful way to positively reinforce the thoughts and messages that inspired you to start along your chosen path, and it will remind you of your passion that is powering your journey.

A helpful and relatively easy way to acknowledge the progress you are making is to take time to celebrate the successes along the way, both the big ones and the small ones. I'm not suggesting that you have a big party every time you achieve a milestone, but to find an appropriate and meaningful way to mark your success. For example, if you've had a small achievement, have a drink of your favorite beverage, and use one of the mantras you created (Insight 7) as a toast to yourself to acknowledge and motivate you to carry on. If you have a larger success, take some time out and do something you'll enjoy, such as go out to dinner with friends to modestly celebrate. If you have a more sizeable success, such as landing a new job or getting that promotion you were trying so hard for, then do something appropriate and mark the achievement such as buying a new outfit for the new job or take a short holiday to rest and rejuvenate before starting the new job—you'll no doubt have more work and responsibility, so some rest before you begin the new role would be in order.

The point I make here is that no matter what the success, just make sure to acknowledge and celebrate the success in a *proportional* way. Such celebrations become positive reinforcement and a reminder of your growing ability and increasing skills; this will encourage you to continue along your path in an energized way.

I remember once when I was working on a number of projects simultaneously, some professional and some personal. It was a very busy period for me but as a self-employed person I felt I needed to take the work when it came along; however, I didn't want to slow the momentum of my personal projects as they were important to me because they brought some happiness and fun into my life.

When I reflect on that time now, I would describe myself as a circus juggler trying to keep one (or maybe even two or three) too many balls in the air. Sometimes on an hourly basis I had to be extremely agile and switch from one mindset to the next just to keep up with deadlines and meeting schedules. After a while, this pressure started to take its toll on me in a destructive way. The grueling pace I was trying to maintain, under the misguided fantasy that I was some sort of superhero, started to affect both my physical and mental health. I was exhausted for weeks, and my body was trying to tell me to slow down, but I was a bit arrogant and just tried to keep up the pace thinking I could manage. Well, I was certainly wrong. In time, I became quite ill and could not get anything done. What made matters worse was that my psychological motivation was also affected, and I just could not find the strength to encourage myself to keep going.

With project deadlines fast approaching, I decided I needed to resume my work but this time I gave myself permission to take breaks more often ... in fact, I insisted upon it and asked some close friend to help make sure I kept this new routine. These breaks were not just for a few minutes ... I decided that every time I made some meaningful "steppingstone" progress, I would do something enjoyable that would refresh, rejuvenate, and reenergize me to keep going. In my case, I love going to the cinema, so whenever I took stock of my progress and realized I had achieved a meaningful milestone, I would go see a new movie that evening. During that period there were many movies I wanted to see but just didn't have the time, so it was a very appropriate reward for myself.

By doing this I gave myself many much-needed breaks and a change of environment that helped to refresh me. This renewed me and put the spring back into my step, and it helped me complete my projects, both professional and personal, much more effectively.

Practice Mindfulness

Many of you may find yourselves feeling overworked and under pressure too, perhaps even to the point of burnout. If you find yourself in this situation, one thing you can try to help the situation is to practice mindfulness. A very simple and basic definition of mindfulness is the ability to be fully present and "in the moment now." Mindfulness provides a keen sense of awareness of where you are and what you're doing, and clarity about where you're going. This clarity and awareness helps you experience a sense of calm and not feeling overwhelmed. Many resources on mindfulness can be found on the Internet and there are many apps that can be downloaded to help you practice mindfulness daily. Take a moment to explore which ones may be helpful and useful to you if you need them.

Learn to Identify Successes

It's one thing to know that you should try and celebrate the little successes along the way, but how will you recognize success when it happens? Remember when you started to visualize your chosen path and planned for action (Insight 5). Perhaps this is a good time to revisit your plan and insert what you would consider successes along the way. Or highlight them if you've already identified them.

It's important to take some time to reflect on what you would consider as successes, especially if your chosen path is one that few people have traveled. Remember there may be no road signs or guideposts along the way if you're carving your own path, a new path (Insight 9), so this is your chance to plant those signposts in case other people choose to follow in your footsteps in the future. To determine if you have made a meaningful achievement, why not reflect on the following questions:

1. How has it enabled you to move forward?
2. How has it helped you?
3. How have you grown from the experience?
4. How will you use the new knowledge/wisdom in the future?

Watch out for the fallacy of thinking everything is a success. It's easy to want to fool yourself every now and then into thinking you've achieved something meaningful even when this may not be the case. This is especially true during times when you may be experiencing challenges or are demotivated or lacking the energy needed to continue the forward momentum. But the moment of truth comes when you are totally honest with yourself about what you've achieved and what is still a work in progress. There's no race to achieve anything, so there is no need for any shame or negative thoughts if you experience a few setbacks every now and then. It's normal and it's to be expected.

Keep an Achievement Journal

A very helpful way to keep track of your successes is to keep an achievement journal. This doesn't have to be anything fancy, just something simple that will encourage you to record your successes as you have them and document your achievements throughout your journey. In time, this will become a great reference to motivate you and provide that much-needed emotional pick-up when things get a bit tough, which is sure to happen from time to time. You can also have a great deal of fun with creating your achievement journal (although don't let the journal become a distraction that delays you from living your leadership lifestyle). For example, instead of writing in your journal, you can create a visual journal, either real or digital (i.e., virtual) by keeping a picture that symbolizes your success every time you have one. Over time, this will grow into a wonderful memory for you as you progress through life and document your successes. As they say, a picture is worth a thousand words, so you're bound to save some time if you keep your journal this way.

Another fun way to keep an achievement journal is to collect a small symbol of your successes every time you have one. One of my friends celebrates her success by buying a small, inexpensive piece of costume jewelry every time she achieves a meaningful milestone. It's a very personal and tangible way she documents her success; every piece in her collection has a story of achievement that goes along with it. The best part about keeping an achievement journal this way is that it combines the act of journaling her success with an act of celebrating her success at the same time … So it's quite efficient. (This routine could get costly over time, but my friend is moderate in what she celebrates and how!)

Don't Let Achievements Fade in Importance

It's surprising how many people find it hard to celebrate their little successes along the way, myself included. From very early in my life, when I achieved certain milestones, I never stopped to acknowledge the success. As I grew older, I found myself intensely focused on my goals and my forward momentum to get across any finish line I had envisioned in my mind. In a way, it was like developing the muscles to succeed at goals, many of which were based purely on necessity, not nice-to-haves.

Unfortunately, I became conscious that with each successive milestone that was reached, which moved me closer and closer to my targeted finish line, I started to become less and less pleased with the progress I had made—and with the steppingstone achievements leading up to that point. As a result, the goal I had set myself seemed to become less important, less meaningful, and less of a success in my mind the closer I came to achieving it. As a result, I would start to shift my focus to think of the next goal I wanted to attempt. I guess you could say that I started to become a bit addicted to goal-setting and perhaps even goal achieving. When I reflect on what kind of harm or damage that may have brought to my own life, it impacted my own well-being and also some close relationships that were very important to me.

I can say with certainty and confidence that there has been disappointment and at times regret because I did not stop to be present in the here and now and in that moment in time to stop, breathe, acknowledge the success, celebrate the success, and more importantly share the success with the people most meaningful in my life at those times.

Celebrate With Others

The joy that comes with sharing your success in a meaningful and proportional way with the people who most probably provided the necessary support and encouragement to get across the finish line and accomplish your goal cannot be overstated. Living a leadership lifestyle means understanding that even though you may choose to carve out your own path and perhaps take the road less traveled or the journey not attempted before … You are never truly traveling alone. There is always someone somewhere supporting and encouraging you, even if you're not aware of it.

Making time to celebrate the successes along the way, both the big and the small, becomes a very meaningful and constructive act both for you and for those who supported you through the journey and helped you achieve your goal. Even though they may not show it for whatever reason, including cultural reasons sometimes, every little success along the way brings a great deal of pride and confidence to you as well as to both your visible and invisible cheerleaders.

These days, when I achieve something, I always try to do a little something special to mark the milestone appropriately and proportionately. Quite recently, I received some good news about a project I was working on for one of my clients. They were pleased with how the project turned out so they had recommended me to others in their network whom they thought could benefit by working with me. This led to two new pieces of business, which I was not expecting but surely welcomed. Taking some time to reflect on this situation and to be present and mindful of what had just happened, I tried to determine what the *real success* was in this situation. After some careful and considered reflection, I determined that the real win was not the two new pieces of business; those were just a pleasant consequence. The real achievement for me was doing a good piece of work that served my client well and surpassed their needs, so much so that they wanted to tell others about me and the high quality of work that I did. This resulted in a very positive working relationship being established that could lead to many more new projects, new experiences, and new, interesting, and meaningful relationships in the future.

To celebrate this success appropriately, I organized a dinner gathering at a local restaurant to say thank you to my clients as well as some colleagues who helped through the project. It was a proportional way to say thank you to those who helped and supported me through the project.

Celebrate the Personal Successes of Others

I've also started doing this more in my personal life as well. But in this context, it's not only for moments to mark my own achievements and success. I attempt to stay informed about the goals and aspirations of my closest friends. Whenever they have a success, I invite them for dinner so we can talk about the journey that led to achieving their goal. This has proved beneficial in several ways. First, it makes us stop and be present, in the moment, to mark the achievement. Second, it gives us the opportunity to talk in more detail about the ups and downs through the journey. On many occasions, I learned new ways to overcome obstacles by taking time to understand how my friends dealt with challenging situations. And third, perhaps the most important benefit of all, it gives us a great reason to meet up and spend some very valuable quality time together, which we sometimes don't get to do because of the hectic pace of our lives.

If you find that the pace of your life is getting more hectic day-by-day as you work hard and strive to achieve your own goals, remember that taking a moment to acknowledge and mark the little successes along the way can be very helpful. Incorporate celebrating successes into your plans as much as possible and you'll find that your leadership lifestyle becomes much more enjoyable.

Leadership Lifestyle Exercise: Acknowledging Success

1. **Identify your successes along the way.** Take a moment to revisit your own plan and identify what you would consider successes along the way. Write them into your plan and think about how you can celebrate the success proportionally once you achieve that goal. Clearly insert that into your plan so it's there to see every time you look at the plan.

2. **Create your achievement journal.** Think about easy, fun, creative, and meaningful ways you could record and document your achievements along the way, both the big successes as well as the steppingstone successes. Now get to work on bringing your achievement journal to life. And go one step further by making your first entry/entries in the journal by thinking of all the little achievements you've already had along the way since you started to read this book.

INSIGHT 12

Be a Student of Life, and a Student for Life

If you were anything at all like me growing up, regardless of the many ups and downs you may have experienced through your school days and regardless of how many great times you might have had, you could not wait to get out of school and start your life! Little did I realize in those days that learning would be a lifelong pursuit, not just for the joy of learning (although I'm quite sure I would not have described it this way back then), but also for the necessity of learning as society continuously progresses.

Living a leadership lifestyle requires you to pursue lifelong learning to stay knowledgeable, informed, flexible, adaptable, agile, resilient, and relevant. Understanding the importance of lifelong learning and the value it brings to your journey toward leadership is one of the most, if not THE most important insights to take note of, especially as we all live in a dynamic and constantly changing and disruptive world.

The lessons from this insight on lifelong learning are the following:

1. Look for new skills to learn.
2. Take advantage of technology.
3. Explore informal learning approaches.
4. Use ongoing learning to be more agile and relevant.
5. Become aware of subconscious learning.

6. Realize you don't know what you don't know.
7. Experiential learning: The lessons of Japan.
8. The learning continues.

Learn New Skills Continually

As you progress in life, you will need new skills to help you navigate the many complexities of modern life, and the fast pace of change means that new skills will be required at an ever-increasing rate. For example, in the last few years, most people have had to learn to become much more comfortable with video meetings and streaming technology as the Covid-19 pandemic severely disrupted the ability to meet family, friends, and colleagues face-to-face. And for those people managing and leading others, yet another set of skills—soft leadership skills such as empathy and team building—had to be harnessed and put into practice as never before.

One of the skills that I had to improve ever since becoming self-employed was time management. After living a busy corporate life for most of my adult years, I found myself in circumstances where I had to do everything by myself. I could no longer afford to just focus on one functional area, such as marketing; I now also had to be the strategy guy, the marketing guy, the sales guy, the operations guy, the administration guy, the IT guy, and most importantly, the guy who actually does the work. Oh, and let's not forget the accountant and chief chaser when clients were late with their payments. It was frustrating and frankly over-whelming at first, but as soon as I found the time to learn how to do these things effectively and efficiently, being self-employed became much more enjoyable.

Take Advantage of Technology

When I was a student many years ago, having an essay or report to complete meant going to the public library and spending hours and hours looking through old books, periodicals, and encyclopedias to gather the information I needed. Usually, the information was dated and not reflective of what was happening in real time. Even early in my career,

I sometimes had to visit a Chamber of Commerce or various trade associations and dig through reams of information to find things relevant for the learning I needed to do, and this was extremely time consuming.

I recall working on a project to market an environmentally friendly marine cleaning product that was used to clean toilets in private yachts. It was such an obscure product that brought to my awareness a whole new industry that I had not even thought of. At the time, the Internet was at its infancy in terms of widespread use, so I had to do all the learning about the product and how best to be successful with the business goals set for me through painstaking research and meetings with many different people who knew different pieces of key information that I needed. It was not just time consuming, but it was exhausting also.

Learning today is easier, quicker, and more accessible than ever before, thanks to technology. While some young people may find it hard to believe, there was life before the Internet and people got by just fine. But as society and technology advances, so does the ability to access new information in new ways that can be delivered through new channels. As a result, our consumption of content has increased at an exponential rate.

This also implies that we have the ability to learn at an exponential rate if we want to—although not everyone does. You can explore any topic you want to by using your favorite search engine such as Google or Bing, as well as other platforms such as LinkedIn Learning and the Khan Academy websites. There are also other online learning platforms that you may not even have considered as learning platforms, such as YouTube, which is great for learning because of the helpful video content to enhance the learning experience. Posts on social media can also be informative. It's almost hard to remember a time before social media was used by the majority of people in society as it's so commonplace and such an essential part of how we learn things in today's world.

Given the rise of the fake-news phenomenon, remember to use some common sense and good judgment with what you learn on the Internet. Verify stories that seem a bit unbelievable or that go against the grain of what most reliable news sources are reporting.

In the past, learning tended to be more onerous; take advantage of the ease of access to information that the Internet provides.

Explore Informal Learning Approaches

Lifelong learning takes place in many different ways. The most common approach is the familiar formal learning, whereby we attend classes at a learning institution to be exposed to new subjects and learn new things that we believe we need or will help us in our lives. People also learn in a formal setting for pure pleasure if they feel a structured way of learning suits them best.

While living a leadership lifestyle includes formal learning, it also includes taking advantage of the many ways to learn informally. Informal learning includes visiting museums and art galleries; the descriptions and explanations attached to the respective exhibits are often filled with fascinating details; streaming podcasts or listen to audio books as you undertake other activities at the same time; talking to new people to learn about their experiences, which is especially impactful if their backgrounds are different from yours; signing up for training courses on topics you simply enjoy, even if those courses have no immediate and obvious usefulness in your daily life; reading online newspapers and e-books or taking online courses through free digital learning platforms. Today, on-demand learning delivery channels let you learn at your own pace when you have the time and mind space to get the most out of your learning.

With so many different ways to learn beyond formal learning environments, there is no reason not to continue your lifelong learning if you really want to. What is most important to live a leadership lifestyle is to be aware of your learning and embrace the fact that you need to continue learning throughout your life in whatever form that learning may come in.

Use Ongoing Learning to Be More Agile and Relevant

New learning in new ways increases your knowledge in two ways. First, you are learning the new subject matter that you are consuming. Second, you are learning how to learn in new ways by being open and trying new learning methods that may not have been available or familiar to you before. If you're a student in higher education, you may have started using various online databases that you access through your institution's library. If you've launched your career, you may be signing up to attend topical conferences and training workshops specific to your chosen field, helping you to stay updated on current developments and learn what's newly emerging in your field.

On a more general level, new knowledge keeps you better informed about the world around you and how society is advancing. This may bring new insights and resources that you can use to live a leadership lifestyle and develop your leadership skills. You also benefit by becoming more agile: lifelong learners can more easily switch from one set of approaches or behaviors to another that may be more appropriate for the situation they're in. By continuing your lifelong learning and staying up to date and relevant in your field of work or expertise, as well as continuously developing and growing your set of skills, you will gain a competitive advantage over those who choose not to pursue their learning.

A timely example of continuous learning in my own life relates to the publishing industry. It was one of my life goals to publish a book. After several failed attempts at getting any traction, I decided to dedicate some time to learning more about publishing as a business. This would help me better understand how to pitch my book ideas by appealing to concepts that publishers would find novel and appealing, rather than just pushing the book I wanted to write. About a year-and-a-half ago, five classmates from an alma mater and I decided to try and write a book that combined the research work we all did for our MA dissertation. We wanted to write for a professional audience, not an academic one: We were all working professionals ourselves and determined that professionals would be the best audience for us to enhance our professional reputations.

I spent some time reading various publishers' websites to understand what they wanted in book proposals and how to structure an effective book proposal. I learned that publishers needed to know what is new or different about your book that reading audiences would find appealing enough to want to buy the book. After all, publishing is a business. I had not thought about this book marketing and sales angle before. Once

I learned about this, I made sure to integrate these sections into our proposal. As a result, our proposal was picked up by a publisher, and the book, *Hidden Challenges: Human Dynamics in Organizational Change and Recovery*, was published in October 2022.

That learning carried forward for me with the proposal I put together for this very book you are reading. The previous learning helped me better understand what makes a book proposal interesting and how to increase the probability of a successful outcome. I am reminded of the competitive advantage I gained through this learning every time I meet someone who tells me they aspire to write a book. I always ask them what they learned about how to get a book published and many of them seem surprised by my question. They are focused on the topic and the book they want to write, but they had not yet learned that there is another side to being successful with this kind of endeavor. I always suggest they spend some time learning about publishing in tandem with their writing to maximize their chances of success.

Become Aware of Subconscious Learning

New knowledge sometimes comes to you when you're not even aware of it. This subconscious learning is another category of learning to add to the formal and informal categories we discussed earlier. Learning can occur consciously or subconsciously. When we purposefully set out on a learning journey, or as I like to refer to it, a learning "adventure," you are making a rational and conscious choice to learn something new. You should achieve some level of success when you set out to learn something new, although this can never be guaranteed unless you put in the hard work required (Insight 7).

However, you may not realize that new experiences that broaden your horizons and help you grow and develop is also a form of learning, although you may not even be aware that learning is taking place. This awareness may only come at a later date. You face a situation or challenge similar to one faced in the past and you find that you're better prepared to deal with the circumstances. At that point you realize that at some point between then and now you acquired a new set of skills and capabilities. The learning occurred in your subconscious, all the while discreetly preparing you for the moment in time when you would need to call upon the new skills in a challenging situation.

A great example of subconscious learning is the impact that engaging in team sports has on your ability to work effectively as part of team on a work-related project. You may not realize it, but the skills you are acquiring during moments that you are seemingly just having fun playing football, basketball, or hockey will help you by embedding within you with a set of skills needed to socially interact with others effectively. Through your "play" you are learning to compete in a friendly way, challenge yourself, and expand your personal boundaries to achieve your full potential, build your confidence for dealing with other people, develop socialization skills for building friendship and support networks, and in time perhaps even building leadership skills that will help you when you take on your first people leadership role.

One of the most important skills to highlight here is effective communication, which is essential for success in all environments, personal or professional. I remember a time in my youth when I played team sports. I was never any good at any of these sports, but that doesn't mean I did not learn a great deal from the experiences I had. By playing team sports and having fun with others, I learned how to communicate clearly and effectively, sometimes in high-pressure/high-stakes situations. This experience directly translated to my working life when I had to lead projects and work with diverse and remotely located teams to achieve our professional objectives with very strict deadlines and limited resources. Another unconscious learning benefit acquired through team sports is the ability to communicate with others who may have very different backgrounds and experiences than you do—whether teammates on your sports team or colleagues at work. During one early work project, I remember having to be creative in how I communicated with some other team members who came from different countries and spoke a different language. Rather than using complicated English words, I sometimes drew images or made sketches of how I thought we could tackle the problem and integrated these into my presentation materials. This was a direct result of remembering the various sketches that were drawn out when determining what plays our sports team might use to get a goal.

You Don't Know What You Don't Know

One of my favorite management models is a leadership knowledge model along the lines of the following:

Simple knowledge matrix

I know what I know	I know what I don't know
I don't know what I know	I don't know what I don't know

There are many different images for this knowledge model, some with different shapes and different sizes of the shapes for the different sections to reflect their prominence, but I think the abovementioned matrix gets across the point I want to make. If you aspire to live a leadership lifestyle, you must develop the ability to be comfortable operating in the bottom right quadrant of the model, accepting that you don't know all the things you don't know, and therefore by extension, there may be an infinite amount left for you to learn. Trying to imagine all that you don't know that you don't know would be a daunting endeavor, however. To incorporate lifelong learning into your life, prioritize the topics, concepts, and learning areas that you think will help you on your journey toward leadership as well as the areas that you will enjoy learning about. If you can find a way to make learning enjoyable, you will see learning as less of a chore and a must-do, and instead reframe your learning as a fun and exciting adventure that is a critical success factor helping you move toward your goal—and grow in the process.

Experiential Learning: The Lessons of Japan

When I reflect on what my own lifelong learning experiences, I feel a sense of gratitude for all the learning opportunities I have had along my own life's path. Of course, there was the formal learning in school when I was a child and later the formal learning I engaged in through the years to acquire three postgraduate degrees. But the lifelong learning experiences that have helped me the most and been most valuable in my life have been those experiential learning opportunities that have challenged me and taken me far outside my comfort zone.

As a young adult, one of the first of these experiences was moving to Japan for my very first full-time job. I've already mentioned my move to Japan and how courage played a role in that experience back in Insight 9, but my time in Japan is also relevant to lifelong learning so allow me to elaborate a bit more on that time here. I was just about 23 or 24 years old at the time and I was so incredibly nervous because I had never even contemplated doing anything like that before in my life. However, I was finding it difficult to get a job just out of school, and wanting to live my own leadership lifestyle, I resolved not to give up and get discouraged at the situation. Instead, I made a choice to take myself out of my comfort zone and move half-way across the world to get a great life experience and one that would hopefully differentiate me and help me build my brand (Insight 3). Little did I know how much that overseas experience would shape me into the person I am today and the leader I am today and help teach me how to live the leadership lifestyle I continue to live decades later.

The experience in Japan taught me how to see things from different angles and to embrace differences as well as similarities among peoples, cultures, countries, and philosophies. I remember having an interesting conversation with some of my Japanese friends about sexuality and nudity when we were making plans to visit a Japanese hot spring (called *onsen*), which is a traditional cultural past time and medically beneficial as well. I was a shy, somewhat coy westerner embarrassed about my body as I had some difficulties with my weight, and also because I have a lot of body hair, which made me stand out compared to most Japanese people. My friends tried to reassure me and when we discussed the topic further in a mature way, they shared their own perspectives that it's only in the western world where nudity is viewed as somewhat taboo and often tied to religion. In their culture, nudity was viewed as natural and respected because of their deep-rooted traditions and customs that had beneficial health outcomes. As a result, any embarrassment was quickly pushed aside in favor of the health benefits. What an epiphany. I had always assumed that everyone had the same views about the body and nudity as we did in the west. I felt so liberated by my newfound knowledge and this not only enabled me to enjoy our visit to the *onsen* that day, but it also helped me keep perspective and deal with a very personal issue that had the potential to negatively affect my self-esteem and, consequently, my own mental health.

Reflecting on that day's events and combining them with other experiences I had while in Japan, I realized that there is no one way of doing things and sometimes there is also no right way of doing things. I learned to accept that there can be many truths and many realities and if I wanted to live a leadership lifestyle, I would have to acknowledge and accept that this might be the situation, even if I did not agree with it. The important thing in these circumstances is to accept and respect that there can be other opinions, and that it's worthwhile to understand those opinions before becoming so rigid in your own perspective that you cannot see the situation in any other way.

That positive yet challenging first overseas experience ended up repeating four more times in my life, and every time I relocated to different countries, even though the scenario was somewhat familiar by then, the challenges remained. I often asked myself why. Surely after the first or second time I moved overseas it should have become a very comfortable and easier experience for me. I finally realized, as my lifelong learning—formally and informally, consciously and subconsciously, and definitely experientially—continued, that the major changes and transformations taking place in my world were not happening on the outside, but rather on the inside. It was me who was changing, growing, and developing each time, always in a constant state of evolution. It was me who was learning new skills and important attributes, such as patience when things don't work out the first time; the ability to laugh at myself when things go wrong because of a silly but understandable mistake I might have made; the ability to take a step back to reflect and see the bigger picture of a situation before prematurely reacting and making things worse; and the importance of nurturing meaningful and genuine relationships throughout life.

The Learning Continues

My lifelong learning became, and continues to be, the catalyst for my personal and professional growth. My continuously developing self-awareness (Insight 2) is a powerful resource enabling me to live my leadership lifestyle, just as I know that your own lifelong learning will become a great resource and enabler for you to live your leadership lifestyle also.

I've been fortunate to have had many different kinds of learning experiences, both formal and informal, conscious, and subconscious. Yet as I write this book in my 50s, I'm in the midst of a new learning adventure: pursuing a doctorate. Feeling the need to carry on my learning yet again, I made the decision to become a student again for the next four to five years. I am filled with a healthy amount of fear, anxiety, worry, and at times a bit of self-loathing wondering why I am putting myself through this lifelong learning experience, very much against the tide of what most people my age would be doing. However, in addition to the negative feelings that surface from time to time, I am also filled with wonder, joy, excitement, purpose, and energy as I am surrounded by others who have a passion and desire for learning. I also welcome the growth that comes from learning how to do research properly and use new tools, techniques, and research methodologies. I am discovering interesting and innovative ways to carry out relevant research that will hopefully have a positive influence and impact on society. My past experience has taught me that what I learn now will help me to continue my personal and professional growth, and enable me to stay more relevant in the future as I live my leadership lifestyle.

When you continue your own lifelong learning, you will see time and time again that learning new things and being able to see things from multiple perspectives will be a valuable tool that enables your ongoing success. You will see challenging situations through a different lens based on a more effective and considered assessment of the circumstances and possible other perspectives to understand what's going on. This, in turn, will help you make better informed and more considered decisions with more clarity.

The importance of lifelong learning is often least appreciated when you're in the moment but becomes a critical success factor when you reflect on what has enabled your success and progress as you journey on your chosen path. To live your own leadership lifestyle, embrace and encounter new experiences that will broaden your horizons, help you develop new and important skills, and navigate the challenges that life brings your way with renewed confidence in your ability to face those challenges and be resilient when you have setbacks every now and then. Always continue your own learning by being a student of life, and a student for life. It will be a rewarding adventure that serves you well and an adventure unlike any you have ever known!

INSIGHT 13

Make the Difficult Choices That Are Needed

While the insights in this book may seem straightforward as you read these chapters, living a leadership lifestyle may require you to change some of your current behaviors, habits, routines, and mindsets. As with all significant change, you may find yourself faced with difficult choices. The following key messages in this insight offer some ways to accept and resolve the difficult choices that may lie ahead:

1. Consciously decide to embrace change.
2. Take a considered approach to overcome dilemmas.
3. Accept that sacrifices sometimes have to be made.
4. Prioritize your choices by changing "No" to "Not Now."
5. Prioritize those who surround you in a meaningful way.

Consciously Decide to *Embrace* Change

One way to overcome the challenge of implementing new and sometimes difficult decisions is to make a conscious choice to adapt and change. Be honest and explicit in your desire to live a leadership lifestyle and to accept whatever may come along in the pursuit. Change of any sort can be difficult, even for people who are accustomed to change and experience it frequently. Think about how you feel about change, especially if some sort of change will be necessary to progress on the path you've carved out for yourself. Will you *endure* the changes that are necessary? Or will you *embrace* the changes required?

How you think and feel about change will have a huge influence on how much you enjoy your journey. If your instinct is to *endure* change, this may be indicative of a negative attitude toward change as the word "endure" evokes a feeling of something painful. If your instinct is to *embrace* change, this may be indicative of being more receptive to change as the word "embrace" evokes pleasant feelings of something positive, like a hug from a loved one. There will often be times when you experience change that disrupts your life. Reacting negatively to such change won't make the situation better and will just prolong the pain. It's helpful in these circumstances to acknowledge the change that has occurred and give yourself permission to be angry, upset, or even uncomfortable for a reasonable period of time. Once that time period has expired, start to think about how the change can actually be positive or used effectively along your chosen path. Consciously making the choice to embrace change and deliberately positioning change as positive may be one of the most challenging steps you have to take to live your leadership lifestyle. However, it is an essential and foundational step that has the power to set you up for success if you can embrace the change effectively or sentence you to failure if you cannot.

Take a Considered Approach to Overcome Dilemmas

There will be other difficult, and sometimes challenging, choices that you have to make along your chosen path. And when these decisions need to be made, you may find yourself in a bit of a conundrum, experiencing a great deal of internal tension because of the task ahead of you. For example, you may be in a situation where you have a choice between two alternatives that have different pros and cons, yet both are somewhat balanced in the benefit you'll receive. How will you make your choice? What criteria will you use to help you decide? There is no guarantee that things will work out the way you hope, so how will you navigate the uncertain and ambiguous circumstances when a decision MUST be made?

Last year I was fortunate to get accepted for doctoral studies into two of the four universities I applied to. Both had excellent reputations, so I made a list of criteria to compare the two to help me make my decision. Tuition fees was one of the criteria. In both schools, I was not successful in getting funding for my studies so examining the financial implications became an important aspect of decision making. School A was about £1,000 less expensive than School B. I also thought about the proximity of both schools. I started to get swayed by the possibility of benefiting from more sleep (an item of high priority for students, well for me at least). School A was about a 10-minute walk from home door-to-door, but school B would take me about 45 minutes to travel to each way.

Then I thought about the maturity and age of the school, which usually is a good indication of how developed it is. School A was in a more mature stage of its development compared to school B, which was not so well established. This meant that things may be a bit more disruptive in school B as the school navigated its own growth until it was in a position to firmly establish its identity and reputation in the marketplace.

Another criterion I concerned was the seniority and profile of the two supervisors who would guide and mentor me through the process of pursuing my doctorate. The supervisors I had lined up in school A were more senior than those I had lined up in school B. When I considered the pros and cons against a set of decision-making criteria, everything was pointing toward me accepting the place at school A. It was cheaper, closer to home, more established, and my supervisors were more senior. Both schools would allow me to study for my doctoral degree and graduate with my PhD.

In the end, I made the difficult choice to accept the place at school B, despite the higher cost, further distance, less established reputation, earlier stage of its maturity as a school, and seniority of supervisory team. Although this might seem a bit odd, I reflected carefully on all the factors involved before making this counterintuitive decision.

One of the key factors for me was the relationship I would develop with supervisors and how available and accessible they would be when I needed their support and guidance. When undertaking a PhD, the relationship with your supervisors, who are essentially your mentors, is a critical success factor that in my opinion trumps everything else. When it was time to accept my place, I realized that the primary supervisor I had at school B was incredibly helpful and had supported me beyond my expectations since the very first time we met—even before I was a student when I was only exploring the possibility of continuing my life-long learning. I felt she had my best interest at heart. For example, when we discussed funding my studies, she was able to identify a research foundation to which I could apply for a scholarship to carry out my research. I pursued this opportunity, and after a competitive application process, I was awarded a full, multiyear PhD scholarship. This scholarship not only covered my tuition costs but also provided a modest monthly stipend so I could truly focus on my studies.

My decision to attend School B proved in many ways to be the right choice, leading to unexpected opportunities beyond my studies. For example, because of my work experience, I was invited by one of the professors at the school to codevelop a leadership course to be delivered to master's degree-level students. I was also invited to get more involved with the executive education team, helping to implement training programs and courses for working executives continuing their education. These are all valuable experiences to have in the academic world and will surely benefit me a great deal in the future.

When I reflect back on my decision, the dilemma I started out with seems to have worked out well. I took a considered and methodical approach not only for resolving my dilemma, setting some criteria as a basis for deciding how to move forward, but also focusing on staying true to myself and determining what would be most important and beneficial for me for the journey forward.

Accept That Sacrifices Sometimes Have to Be Made

Another difficult choice that you may face in living a leadership lifestyle is the decision to sacrifice something you don't necessarily wish to lose. For example, a leader may want to keep an exceptional employee in his business unit although there is an opening somewhere else in the company that would be perfect for this person's career. The leader has a choice: to say nothing to the employee about the open position and keep that employee in the team, or to encourage the employee to apply for the position and even offer support by making a recommendation, even though the outcome would be the loss of an excellent team member. A true leader would choose the second option. The development of people is one of the hallmarks of good leadership. While you might lose a good employee and team member in the short term, in the long term you are helping build your credibility as a leader.

In your own daily life, you may really want something—for example, a new luxury car that costs more than you've ever paid for a car, or a vacation to a sunny beach destination to escape the horror of a freezing winter. You may want to rush out without any further thought and get what you want as you think of the instant gratification it will bring you—and well, let's face it ... you deserve it don't you? However, if you always succumb to your spontaneous desires and whims, you might be taking backward steps along your chosen path. Is the expensive purchase what you really need at this moment? Think about the journey that you visualized, planned, and have now acted on by starting to take your first steps down that path (Insight 5). Then think about how the current choice under consideration will affect your rate of progress and impact your overall goal. If there is very little negative impact, then go ahead and treat yourself. But if there could be a negative impact that has the potential to set you back significantly, then take a moment and consider what choice you want to make and why. Then proceed with caution, but also with confidence in knowing why you're making that decision and how it will impact you. Then own that decision by acknowledging and accepting the consequences that could potentially come along with it.

I remember the time I believed I was ready to buy my first home. It was a daunting experience to say the least, and given my personal circumstances at the time, let's just say that it was a truly aspirational goal. My family might be able to help a bit with a down payment, but nothing beyond that. There were no government schemes to help me then as there are now for first-time buyers. I'm not sure if it was a blessing, a curse, or a situation of purgatory, but with my financial situation at the time, I fell into the in-between category of people who couldn't afford a home and people who were financially stable enough to not qualify for any special financial assistance whatsoever.

I was angry at first. I had worked hard all my life and always tried to be financially responsible and a good citizen, and now when I needed some help it was not available to me the way many others were able to benefit from. By the way, I still fall into that in-between category even decades later, but I've let all the anger go! In that situation, with the purchase of my first home, I allowed myself some time to get over the frustration brought on by my personal circumstances, then started to think about ways to be clever in order to continue to pursue my goal and not give up in despair.

I started with mapping out all my financial inflows, the cash that was coming in, and then mapped out all my financial outflows, the cash that was being spent. After seeing the result, I had a bit of a rude awakening and realized just how much I was spending on relatively unnecessary and unimportant things that I could easily cut down on and perhaps even do without. I also saw how much was being squandered away because of thoughtless choices I was making, fully within my ability to influence.

As a result, I sat down and created a personal budget, setting some realistic limits for spending on things I truly needed to avoid hardship in life, but also allowing myself a few indulgences so I could enjoy life. I made sure to put some limits on these indulgences and very consciously decided that any excess savings would be directed to my home-buying fund, which I newly created to help accelerate my progress.

At first, adjusting to these new constraints was understandably a bit difficult. I used some helpful mantras I created to help me maintain the discipline (Insight 7) I required to make progress on my chosen path. In this case, that mantra was "Homeward bound." It was nothing new, creative, revolutionary, or particularly insightful. But to me those were the most meaningful two words at that time of my life. I managed to stay the course and when the time actually came to buy the property, my first home, I found I had saved up more that the required minimum for a down payment, which benefited me by opening up more possibilities for mortgages with preferential interest rates, so I would save more money in the long term. I took the time to celebrate my little success along the way of my life journey (Insight 11) in an appropriate and proportional way, because that success was all the more meaningful to me because of the hard work I had to put in to achieve it. I bought myself a very special key chain that would come to hold all my home keys; I still have that key chain years later as a reminder of the time I had to make some difficult choices and the benefit that came my way by doing so.

Prioritize Your Choices by Changing "No" to "Not Now"

Another way to deal with difficult choices is to reframe them altogether. Often when people are faced with making difficult choices, there seems be a default mindset that it's an all-or-nothing choice. But that doesn't have to be the case at all. If you're in this situation and you're finding it hard to say no to something that seems important to you at that moment, see how you feel if you changed the "no" to a "not right now." Remember that there are times when what may seem *important* to you may not necessarily be *good* for you at that moment depending on what goals you've set for yourself. By saying "not now" instead of "no," you lessen the emotional impact of setting something aside by acknowledging its importance to you, but perhaps giving it a lower priority than something else that will have a more positive impact in your life. This also becomes a reminder to you that even by not indulging in something spontaneously, you are doing something positive for yourself overall. Later, after you've achieved the higher priority goal, you can come back to this one and revisit the situation to determine if it's still important to you or whether you've moved on.

Living a leadership lifestyle is not about making meaningless sacrifices that have the potential to take the joy out of life, but it is about temporarily deferring instant pleasure and gratification at times when needed in order to pursue and achieve your higher priority goals. Choosing to forego something and make a temporary sacrifice can be difficult, but the ability to develop this skill and mindset will benefit you in the long run by helping you achieve your goals sooner.

I remember one year that I received a larger-than-usual bonus at the end of the company's fiscal year. It was quite some time ago and I was more materialistic than I am today. I had already bought my home and set some ambitious goals for myself to pay down the mortgage every year, hoping not to be burdened with a lifetime of mortgage debt. But because the bonus came unexpectedly, I thought of the added money as, well, like a bonus! At that time, I was captivated by Swiss watches and had my heart set on buying myself a fancy designer Swiss watch costing thousands of dollars. It was totally unnecessary and unimportant in the grand scheme of my life, but it was important to me ... A very personal and discrete symbol of my success. I found myself trying to convince myself that spending all that money on a fancy watch was the right thing to do. But in the end, I trusted instincts and listened to my inner voice (Insight 4) and waited a while before making an impulse purchase. This gave me time to think carefully about how to apply my unexpected bonus in a constructive and meaningful way. I decided in the end to make an additional capital payment toward paying down my mortgage instead of buying that fancy Swiss watch.

At first, I was a bit sad about the whole thing. However, the following year interest rates increased somewhat unexpectedly due to the economic climate and my mortgage payment would have surely increased to a point that could have created some stress for me. But because I had made that extra lump-sum payment with the bonus money, thus bringing down my regular mortgage payments, there was only a marginal increase in my payments that year and I was able to weather the storm.

My decision to forego the Swiss watch and the resulting beneficial outcome when interest rates increased taught me a valuable lesson; for the following few years, I paid down as much of my mortgage as I could with my bonus money. Before I knew it, my payments decreased to the point that I was able to save up for that fancy Swiss watch and buy it after all. I had never said "no" to my fancy Swiss watch. I had simply said, "not now," and made the difficult choice I needed to make in that moment to get further ahead with more meaningful and higher priority goals in life.

If living your leadership lifestyle is keeping you from moving forward along the path you chose to be on, then perhaps it's time to take stock of things and determine what changes may be necessary and what difficult choices you may have to make in order to move in the direction you want. Once this is done and you've implemented any changes that are necessary, you will find in no time at all that what you may have thought was going to be a difficult and painful change to make is a lot easier than you thought. The reason: you've been able to adapt to your new circumstances by embracing change, resolving dilemmas in a considered way, prioritizing who surrounds you in a meaningful way, accepting that sacrifices must be made some time, and by prioritizing your choices rather than giving things up totally. Even though you may be deferring some of your immediate pleasure and comfort in the short term, you're working hard toward your higher priority goals, and you can feel proud of yourself for achieving your goals sooner and taking accountability for your own success (Insight 1).

Prioritize Those Who Surround You in a Meaningful Way

The most difficult of choices and decisions to make may arise when they involve other people. You may have to choose between people who are more constructive to be around during certain times in life or people who may be less so.

Allow me to clarify this somewhat controversial point. I am not suggesting in any way that you cut people out of your life and only include people in your life selectively if they can enable you to further your goals. That would clearly NOT be the way to live a leadership lifestyle as it reeks of self-serving exploitation and selfishness—the antithesis of what living a leadership lifestyle is all about.

That said, keep a healthy perspective on the relationships you build and develop with various circles. You may have to reconcile the positives and the negatives of these relationships with the circumstances in which you find yourself so that you can determine which relationships might better enable you to progress on the path to achieving your stated goals. If you are in a situation where you make this difficult choice, nurture these goal-oriented relationships as much as you can, while not ignoring the other relationships in your life.

There is also much to learn from the relationships that you determine may be less helpful in that point in your life. Remember to be mindful of how you prioritize your relationships; living a leadership lifestyle requires that you treat everyone fairly, compassionately, and most of all with the respect and dignity that you yourself would want to be treated with.

As I started studying for my doctorate, I had some wonderful close friends whom I would have loved to spend more time with on a regular basis during my first year. However, because of the academic demands placed on me, it was hard to find the time to get together with them; most of my time during this period in my life is spent with other students or faculty members on campus in a formal learning environment that isn't always "fun." But that is what is needed to help me progress and so I have to prioritize my studies.

Because the people in my closest circles are very important to me, I still deliberately nurture these relationships by staying in touch with them when I am not able to meet in person. I send e-mails and text messages, and I even make sure to telephone them to check in and see how they are doing, which acts both as a reminder and a reaffirmation of how important the friendships are to me.

Leadership Lifestyle Exercise: Dealing With Difficult Choices

Take a moment to think about the path that you're currently on. Revisit the earlier aspirations that you visualized, planned, and acted on. How are you coming along on your journey? Are you on course? If you're having challenges making progress, think about why that might be and write it down. Now take a few minutes to allow yourself to be frustrated, and then get that frustration out of your system. You may even have to step away from this leadership lifestyle exercise and come back to it at a later time. Once your negative emotions are out of your system, try and think creatively about how you can work around any obstacles you're facing and what difficult choices you may need to make to circumvent those obstacles. Now think about how you can implement some of those changes with the least amount of disruption in your daily life and get to work making those changes happen. In no time at all, you'll find you've adapted and you're back on course. Often, the anticipation of negative impact brought on by any change creates more anxiety than the actual changes themselves.

Conclusion

Living a leadership lifestyle means making deliberate decisions and taking action that has been carefully considered and planned. Of course, there is also room for spontaneity and a bit of fun—everything has its place although moderation and balance is an important key to success. The 13 insights in this book provide a structured game plan for living a leadership lifestyle and achieving success and happiness in your personal and professional lives.

Insight 1 focused on the theme of taking accountability for your own success. It's easy to get stuck in a downward negative spiral and feel as if the world is sometimes against you. Shift your mindset and own up to the reality that you are accountable for your success. Don't wait around for life to happen to you; instead, do what you can to move forward.

Insight 2 discussed the importance of self-awareness, which is key to becoming a good leader. A deeper knowledge of your personal strengths, developmental areas, values, personal drivers, and key motivators helps you to make decisions and take action that aligns with who you are at your core. Developing a genuine identity profile in the leadership lifestyle exercise is a great way of taking stock of who you are and becoming more self-aware.

Insight 3 highlighted the importance of building and protecting your personal brand. Living a leadership lifestyle means making a choice to stand for something important to you and regardless of what that may be. Your personal brand becomes a calling card as you establish your reputation as a leader through your actions and behaviors in daily life. Investing time to complete the leadership lifestyle exercise "Build Your Personal Brand" will get you started on the journey to defining yourself as a leader.

Insight 4 was about trusting your instincts and listening to your inner voice. The feelings you have and the thoughts you hear in your minds are important bits of data that you can translate into information to steer you on your course. Living a leadership lifestyle means not just pushing those pieces of information emerging from your instincts and inner voice aside, but rather acknowledging them, reflecting on them to find meaning, integrating them into the circumstances in which you find yourself in the moment, and using them as a compass to help you on your way.

Insight 5 was about shifting the focus from just thinking about living a leadership lifestyle to taking your first action steps along your journey to leadership. It's important to first visualize your goals and plan your steps, before taking considered action that propels you in the direction of your goals. Remember, "A goal without a plan is just a wish" and "A plan without action is just a regret."

Insight 6 acknowledged that achieving goals is not always easy and often comes with risks that can stop you in your tracks. Risk itself, however, is neutral, neither good nor bad. It's how you identify and mitigate the risks you face on a regular basis that helps you become successful. Living a leadership lifestyle means accepting that risk will always be present; you have to determine how to deal with those risks effectively in order to move forward.

Insight 7 highlighted the importance of resilience in achieving a leadership lifestyle. There are no easy routes or short cuts to success. Reframing the challenges you face, not hesitating to ask for help, and using personal mantras to encourage you when obstacles and setbacks threaten to slow you down or stop you completely are valuable tools for overcoming the difficult times that may lie ahead.

Insight 8 was a reminder that on the road to leadership, failure is an opportunity in disguise. Through failure you learn valuable lessons and gain key insights that will help you later. Failure also helps build the resilience and confidence to face challenging situations in the future. Progress occurs one step at a time. Remember that experience brings knowledge, knowledge brings wisdom, wisdom brings success.

Insight 9 encouraged you to show courage and to carve your own path. It's your journey to leadership, and the things you experience along the way will be unique to you. Don't be afraid to try new things, meet new people, take the road less traveled, and have experiences that will broaden your horizons. The Carving Your Own Path leadership lifestyle exercise will help set you off in the right direction and navigate the roads less traveled.

Insight 10 discussed the sometimes cyclical and chaotic path that you may experience on your journey to leadership and success. What's important to remember is that there is not one truth, nor one answer for everyone. It's up to you to define your own definition of progress and success. If you are willing to let go of the past, accept that progress is non-linear, and anticipating roadblocks and preparing for them before they even appear, you will find yourself enjoying the journey.

Insight 11 highlighted one of the most important lessons for living a leadership lifestyle: Take time to celebrate the successes, both big and small, that you have on your journey. By reminding yourself of just how far you've come along your chosen path, celebrations of successes build your self-confidence and self-esteem and keep you motivated. The leadership lifestyle exercise of keeping an achievement journal will help you to record your successes and be a great keepsake of the progress you've made.

Insight 12 highlighted the importance of lifelong learning. Continuing your formal and informal learning helps build new skills and capabilities that keep you relevant in a rapidly evolving world. Living a leadership lifestyle means recognizing that the learning must never stop, because there is so much that you don't know. Developing the mindset for continual lifelong learning will help you maintain forward momentum in your life as you cope and adapt to the inevitable changes ahead.

Insight 13 encouraged you to be prepared to make the unavoidable difficult choices that life will place before you. Achieving a leadership lifestyle will necessitate compromise and sacrifices. Look for the compromise before having to make a sacrifice. If a sacrifice is necessary and worthwhile, move forward with the difficult decision. In many situations, a sacrifice is only temporary: you pass on what you want for now but can revisit them later if they're still a priority for you.

These 13 insights are a guide for achieving success in life and work. However, it's important that *you* define the success you want and the path you want to follow. Leadership begins with accountability and that applies for your personal life as much as your professional life. One of the core lessons of this book is to carve your own path.

Remember also that life is a marathon, not a sprint. Plan your next steps carefully, make considerate decisions when decisions must be made, but it's okay if you're not able to map out the entire journey for there are inevitable opportunities and setbacks along the way that cannot be planned ahead of time. The best you can do is to know who you are and to have the courage to take the next steps that align with your values.

So now, it's up to you. Are you ready to take your first steps on your journey to living a leadership lifestyle? If you are struggling or find yourself hesitating to make the changes that could lead to more happiness and success, take some time to reflect on your situation and what might be stopping you or slowing you down. Use skills such as reframing to realistically appraise any obstacles you may be facing. Think about what resources you may need to get you started along your journey and then plan out ways to acquire those resources. And be ready to ask for help. Carving your own path does not mean going it alone. Ask for help if and when you need it. Don't be afraid to show your vulnerabilities and talk openly about your challenges. People will help you if they can.

If you really have a passion for living a leadership lifestyle, you will draw the courage you need to take your first steps on the journey from the fire deep within your heart. Remember, your passion will power your progress; and your heart will carry your feet.

About the Author

Ross Emerson is a leadership and executive coach, consultant, and advisor with over 30 years of professional history drawing from international experience in Canada, Japan, United Kingdom, Monaco, and India. He owns and operates a private coaching, consulting, and advisory practice serving clients around the globe under his personal brand, Ross Emerson Ltd.

Ross is passionate about developing people and has a penchant for working with aspiring leaders at junior, senior, executive, and board levels. During a successful career spanning over 30 years, Ross held senior roles in financial services strategy, operational risk management, learning and development, global payments, wealth management, and enterprise leadership. In 2021, Ross was invited by the National Institute of Organisation Dynamics, Australia, to present his research at their annual Symposium themed "Not Knowing and Coming to Know: Methods of Inquiry in Unconscious (Hidden) Dynamics in Organisations." Also in 2021, Ross was nominated for an Ontario Premier's Award for success in business. In 2013 and 2014, Ross won the Royal Bank of Canada's Private Banking Gold Award given to the top enterprise leaders across Canada. Prior to that in 2009 and 2011, Ross won the Barclays Chairman's Award for Individual Contribution to the Monaco and to the Europe regions, respectively. In 2002, Ross was privileged to be part of the World Youth Day team organizing the visit of Pope John Paul II to Toronto. In 2003, Ross relocated to England and worked as deputy fundraising director at the Duke of Edinburgh's Award and, after several years, he was headhunted by the National Youth Theatre of Great Britain to join its Executive Committee as development director.

Ross has served as nonexecutive director on the boards of two UK charities in the past and served on the board for the Canadian Centre for Diversity between 2012 and 2014 as chair of its Development Committee as well as being treasurer for a short period. Currently, Ross serves as a director and co-chair of a property complex where he provides strategic oversight and guidance for the management of over 100 homes as well as commercial businesses.

Ross holds an Honors BA degree in Politics from Western University, a Graduate Certificate in International Business from Seneca College, an MBA from the Schulich School of Business, and an Executive Master in Change degree (distinction) from INSEAD's program on organizational culture and change management. In October 2021, Ross commenced a PhD in Management Studies at King's College. He was awarded a full, multiyear PhD scholarship by the T. Ritchie Rodger Research Foundation connected to the British Psychological Society to carry out his research in the leadership, clinical organizational psychology, and organizational behavior arenas.

Ross is a member of the Academy of Management, the European Group for Organization Studies, and is certified in the Hogan Leadership Suite of psychometric tools. He previously completed his UK Investment Management Certificate, the Canadian Securities Course, and held the personal financial planner designation in Canada. In his spare time, Ross enjoys traveling, cooking, soft jazz, and going to the cinema.

Index